'*Secret Places of West Dorset* elegantly invites us to explore this magical and at times transcendental area. The book achieves a literary feel without ever being difficult or a chore to read. The writing feels very free, moulding personal experiences with literary, historical and folk references.'

Dorset Echo

'It goes off the beaten track to cover folklore, curiosities, legends and history as well as churches, ancient trackways and enigmatic stones.'

Bridport News

'This little gem of a book demonstrates just how much there is to be discovered west of Weymouth. … Some of these places are atmospheric simply because they are wild and empty; others have faint traces of some lost and mysterious past. Well written and informative, the book is beautifully illustrated with colour photographs and the author's watercolours.'

Steve Marshall, Fortean Times

'A clear to understand book with many colourfully illustrated walks and useful information to make your day out easier.'

South West Connection

'Even if you don't go out to enjoy the suggested walks, you can cosy up in your armchair and explore in your mind Dorset's folklore, curiosities, legends and history. … The many photographs and author's own paintings help to illustrate the rare beauty of this part of the county.'

Dark Dorset

Secret Places of West Dorset

Louise Hodgson

*A sentiment which frequently occurs,
particularly it seems to English poets and mystics,
alludes to some intangible Mystery
concealed within the landscape*

(John Michell)

Roving
Press

© 2011 Louise Hodgson

Published by Roving Press Ltd
4 Southover Cottages, Frampton, Dorset, DT2 9NQ, UK
Tel: +44 (0)1300 321531
www.rovingpress.co.uk

First published 2011 by Roving Press Ltd
Reprinted 2012

ISBN: 978-1-906651-091

British Library Cataloguing in Publication Data
A catalogue record for this book is available from the British Library

Artwork by Louise Hodgson
Photographs by Roving Press and Louise Hodgson
Map and cover design by Roving Press

Front cover photo: ruined chapel in the wood near Abbotsbury
Back cover photos: view across South Warren Hill near Melplash; lion's head water spout in Stoke Abbott
Frontispiece photo: Powerstock Common

The quote on the title page is from *The View Over Atlantis* by philosopher and writer John Michell

Set in 11.5/13 pt by Beamreach (www.beamreachuk.co.uk)
Printed and bound by Henry Ling Ltd, at the Dorset Press, Dorchester, DT1 1HD.

To the late John Michell
who encouraged when right to do so
and gave kindly advice when my footsteps faltered.
This book is lovingly dedicated.

Contents

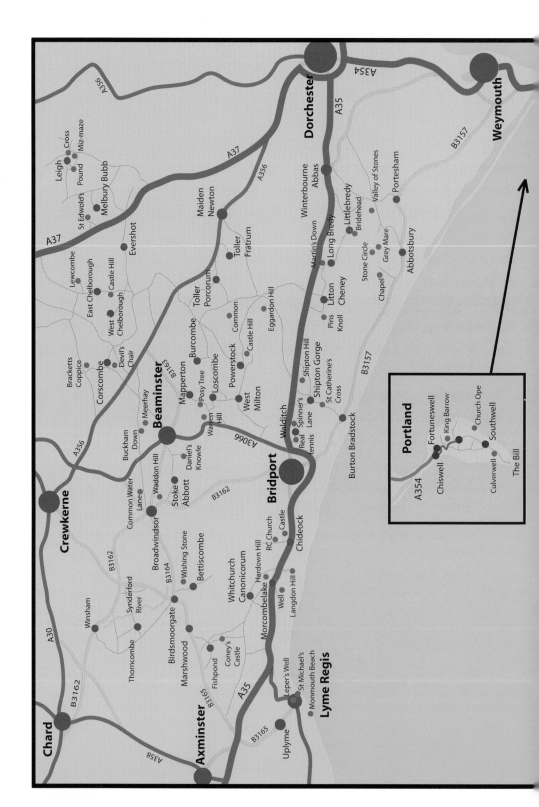

About the Author

Louise Hodgson has spent most of her life in the West Country and currently lives in West Dorset. Over the years she has walked and explored this part of the county and some of her most intriguing discoveries are in this book. She has been published in *The Literary Review*, *City Canticle Magazine* (San Francisco), *The Equinox* and other periodicals and her artwork has been exhibited in the West Country and London. She has appeared on television – on BBC *Points West*, discussing her pilgrimage through the Cotswolds, Wiltshire, Dorset and Somerset, accompanied by a pack-pony and greyhound, and on ITV *Network 7*, discussing the importance of the Midsummer Solstice. She has taught 'Landscape and Spirituality' at Frome College, Somerset, and currently runs a tour company called *Secret Landscape Tours*. You may contact Louise about her writing, art and tours via the website www.secretlandscapetours.com.

Acknowledgements

Many people have provided the insight that, over the years, has helped subtly inform this book. The late John Michell, author and mystic and one of my oldest friends, was a guide and mentor, and to his far-reaching wisdom I am hugely indebted. My companion in my youth, the late Martin Doyle, introduced me to the poetry of the landscape, with evening walks over the Wiltshire Downs, a lurcher at our side. I am grateful to the Marquis of Bath, then Lord Weymouth, who provided us with a cottage in beautiful Horningsham, a village on the Wiltshire/Somerset border where my love of the countryside was cultivated. Mark Palmer, the aristocratic gypsy who travelled all over Britain in a barrel-topped horse-drawn wagon, camped near us for a while, fuelling my enthusiasm for the itinerant life. This enthusiasm took shape some years later when I too took to the road, with pack-pony and greyhound. Thanks to the two Romany men, Tuck and Giles, both living with a real kinship to the land, who shared some of their wisdom with me.

Merrily and Patrick Harpur have been most valuable friends over recent years. Their vision and high sensibility have helped refine my perception and strengthen my resolve. Thanks to Neil Judd for sharing his experience of the Black Dog; to Susann Palmer who provided helpful advice regarding the Culverwell Mesolithic site; and to the various people whose valuable snippets of information have added to this book.

How to Use This Book

Places appear alphabetically for ease of location, with clear directions to get you there by car/bike, including Ordnance Survey map number and grid references. Some of the locations are one-off places to visit and enjoy, others have ideas for stimulating walks. It is essential to carry the appropriate OS map for the area (OS Explorer Maps 116, 117 or OL15; or Landranger maps 193 or 194) so you can devise walks to suit your abilities.

For the more remote sites there are also indications of nearby 'refreshment' establishments or locations. However, none of these are sponsored entries and in no way form an endorsement by the author or publisher.

Introduction

West Dorset is quite different from the rest of the county because of its variety of countryside and special topography, varied hues, textures, contours and symmetry. Old farms, held by the same family for generations, are part of this landscape, as are ancient tiny fields, a relic from Celtic times. The villages and towns have, as everywhere, both old buildings and new, but there are enough of the old to confirm that the 'soul' of the place still exists. Sites of great antiquity rest here – stone circles, stone monoliths, chambered tombs and other artefacts from the Neolithic onwards. At Martin's Down above Long Bredy, a small village in the Bride Valley, there is a massive cemetery to the prehistoric dead. The memory of those far-off times subtly pervades the landscape, with traces of flint, bone, mound and earthen bank. It is remarkable that these fragile tombs and ritual places have survived so long. Certainly many have vanished, ploughed out or the stones pillaged for building, but enough remains to give us a tangible link with our distant past.

I sometimes let intuition lead my walks and often find myself in some wonderful and mysterious places. There are landscapes in the little things – an ancient thorn tree growing around an old rock, swathes of bluebells in a wood, moss growing on a fallen branch. I have seen many odd occurrences in my explorations, one of the strangest and most wonderful being that of the magical hare, seen in a valley above Uploders. In the hot summer of 1976 I travelled with a pack-pony and greyhound from Stow-in-the-Wold in the Cotswolds, journeying through Wiltshire, east Somerset and Dorset and along the coast to Lyme Regis, eventually ending my journey back at Butleigh near Glastonbury. It was a pilgrimage of sorts, exploring ancient track-ways and allowing myself the freedom to relate to the land, letting the influences of the natural world guide me. On a warm late afternoon in early September I arrived at Uploders near Bridport. A kind farmer allowed me to camp in his orchard and after loosing the pony I took my greyhound bitch Fern up a track onto the open hills above the village, in the hope of catching a rabbit for the pot. Strolling along, I met two gypsy men with lurchers and we decided to walk together. In a way we were kindred spirits, each with a hunting dog and the shared affinity of travelling people, though my travelling was more of a novice compared with that of the Romany. One of the men, Giles Cooper, said he was a 'rank' Romany, in other words he had pure gypsy blood. He was based in the Sturminster Newton area but travelled a fair distance with his pair of lurchers, poaching hares. The Somerset Levels around Langport was a favourite hunting ground, with plentiful large fast hares. As we talked we were also looking around for small game, and as we were walking above a blind valley, a valley ending in a curve of the hillside, Giles suddenly exclaimed, 'Gor, look at that deer surrounded by all them hares!' I looked and saw about a dozen hares partially surrounding a much larger animal. To our amazement, we saw that it was not a deer but an enormous giant hare, a King or Queen Hare. We stood and watched in reverent silence. Hares don't normally congregate at any time other than the spring mating season, so to see such a large company in September was extremely unusual, and, with the addition of the presiding figure of the giant hare, was an extraordinary experience. We didn't stay beyond a few minutes because there was a shared deep-down feeling that we were intruding on something magical, rare and private. We carried on our walk slowly and quietly, our dogs leashed.

The hare is an animal steeped in folklore. Large females are known as doe hares, but whether this term encompasses anything as large and somehow supernatural as the hare we saw is questionable. I have never seen such a sight mentioned in any book nor had I heard, until recently, of anyone else who had seen anything similar. When I recounted this tale to some people in the summer of 2010, one of them, a man in his early forties, was triggered into remembering that as a youth he too had seen a giant hare, alone at the edge of a wood.

It is the strangest adventure to have a first-hand experience of something so mythic as this magical hare, but Dorset is full of supernatural and bizarre tales, some of which are recounted in this book. There is a plethora of fascinating history, folklore and legends connected with many of the places we visit. Old Dorset has a wealth of fairy-lore and descriptions of encounters with strange beings are all part of the inner life of the landscape. Folk memory is a precious resource still held by some of the old country people. I have learned a lot from talking and listening to them.

This book is a collection of my personal favourite places in West Dorset. I have tried to avoid the well-known elements, preferring the less familiar jewels, for one of its keynotes is *exploration*. Many of the places described are tricky to get to – lanes narrow and pot-holed, paths and tracks often wet and muddy (best tackled in wellingtons). Yet they are worth seeking out and you will be rewarded by experiencing places of rare beauty and charm. Then hopefully inspiration will lead you to inquire further and make your own special discoveries.

ABBOTSBURY
Ruined Chapel in the Wood

OS maps: Explorer OL15 or Landranger 194

Grid refs: Parking SY557872, Chapel SY556878

Directions: Head west out of Abbotsbury towards Bridport on the B3157, and after approx. 1 mile, at the top of the hill turn right down a small lane signposted Ashley Chase. Park after approx. 0.5 miles just before the lane forks right and becomes private. Take the track to the left (northwest) and after 800 m, at the bottom of the hill, a footpath on the right leads into Chapel Coppice. You will find the Chapel approx. 300 m into the woods.

Nearby refreshments: Abbotsbury, Swyre, Puncknowle and West Bexington

The farm and lands of Ashley Chase, lying northwest of Abbotsbury, were given to the Cistercian monks from Netley Abbey near Southampton by local landowner William of Litton in 1246. The land was gifted in exchange for perpetual prayers being said for William and his family. Gifts such as this were quite common in the mediaeval era; salvation of the soul did not come cheap. Until the dissolution of Netley Abbey in 1538, monks and lay brethren would have farmed Ashley as a secluded outpost of the abbey. A small chapel, dedicated to St Luke, was built near the farm for the use of the community there. St Luke was a Greek-speaking

Syrian from Antioch and companion to St Paul in the 1st century AD. He was an Apostle and a physician and historian. The fact that he was a Gentile was unusual but did not diminish his stature within the Jewish brotherhood.

With the dissolution of the abbey, the monks scattered, their abbey dismantled. The chapel would have seen occasional use over a hundred years or so, but as people died or left the area the building became increasingly less frequented. Abandoned, apart from the odd solitary pilgrim, the mediaeval chapel deteriorated as the years passed, becoming increasingly ruinous. The farm and land passed through various owners until 1925 when it was purchased by Sir David and Lady Milne-Watson. The couple built a large house near the farm that they named Ashley Chase. They also took an interest in the chapel. Woodland surrounded the small areas of wall and western gable, all that remained of the chapel, and even that was close to collapse. Efforts were made to shore up the gable and it still stands.

Something in the peace and history of the chapel must have deeply appealed to the Milne-Watsons, so much so that they are buried here. Their simple headstones in the centre of the fragmented nave are in sympathy with what remains here. These two people have left a testament to their character. They have gently aligned themselves to this small, sanctified area and

given it their blessing and with that they have also bestowed a wider blessing. They have blessed the idea of continuation. A place once holy can always continue to be so if the will is there. There is a heightening quality in hidden, undisturbed places, particularly if those places are prehistoric temple sites or of an ecclesiastical nature, as here. This chapel has been a building charged by prayer and devotions for over 300 years and the benediction that is implied remains.

Painting 1: Looking through the ruined, tree-framed archway of the woodland chapel towards the altar.

ABBOTSBURY
Kingston Russell Circle, Grey Mare and Valley of Stones

OS maps: Explorer OL15 or Landranger 194

Grid refs: Circle parking SY588867, Kingston Russell Stone Circle SY578878, Grey Mare long barrow SY584871, Valley of Stones SY596873

Directions: Take Back Street northeast from the centre of Abbotsbury village. Follow this lane up the hill for about 1 mile, past the disused Lime Kiln, then just after a sharp right-hand bend (near the Ridgeway path) turn sharp left. Park respectfully on the verge, before the lane becomes private. Do not cross the cattle grid, but of the three available paths take the central one heading northwest. After 500 m you can take a 100-m detour west to the Grey Mare and Her Colts long barrow. This is reached by a stile on the left of the path and is visible in the second field, when viewed from the gate. Retrace your steps to the main footpath and continue in a northwesterly direction again for a further 1 km. The Kingston Russell Stone Circle, named after the nearby manor, is well maintained and clearly defined in the field. For the Valley of Stones, drive back to the main lane, turn left towards Hardy's Monument and park on the verge approx. ½ mile east. The Valley is signed to your north.

Nearby refreshments: Abbotsbury and Portesham

The Russell's were a Norman family who for upwards of 200 years held the manor of Kingston Russell in sovereignty to the King. Over the centuries the village declined, the population dwindling, with many being lost to the Black Death. The little mediaeval Chapel of St James, which had served the small population well over the years, slowly disintegrated and disappeared and very few buildings were left by the early 17th century when the Michel family, who were originally from East Devon, first built Kingston Russell House. In the 18th century the house was let to Joseph Hardy and his wife and in 1769 Thomas Masterman Hardy was born there. Thomas Hardy became Admiral Hardy, later to win acclaim at the Battle of Trafalgar and be commemorated by the Hardy Monument, a landmark that can be seen for miles as it stands on the heights of nearby Black Down. This area is one of many in the locality that contains prehistoric monuments and the ancient track that runs along the crest of the hills is lined with barrows that show up on the skyline.

Tenants Hill, which rises above Lower Kingston Russell, now little more than a farm, has a number of important prehistoric sites including a tumulus, enclosure and hut circle. As the area is approached, the most immediately visible site is a stone circle of fallen sarsen stones, the Kingston Russell Stone Circle.

The circle, which is actually rather oval, has a diameter of at least 18 m (60 ft) and dates from the late Neolithic period, having been erected around 2000 BC. Stone circles are places of ritual activity rather than burial sites, but what that activity was no one quite knows. Some people believe certain stones in a circle are aligned to the midsummer sunrise, or have links with some of the astrological patterns of the stars, such as the Pleiades. Others feel there might have been sacrifices here, although no firm evidence has been found to suggest this. To the ancients the stones were imbued with life, they were 'living'. Notably, the circle is situated at the junction of five paths.

These ageless, sometimes huge stones used in prehistoric ritual sites pose a conundrum and posit many questions. For example, why were the Pembrokeshire bluestones transported to Stonehenge? Was it to take on the power of a defeated tribe – taking their sacred stones, their strength, their memories, their energy? Or was it to establish a connection with the area the stones came from? Maybe the subtle frequency of the bluestones was needed to augment the magical currents of the embryonic Stonehenge, or possibly the people who erected Stonehenge came originally from the Pembrokeshire area and the bluestones contained the spirits of their ancestors, brought with them to provide continuity and a living link with ancestral homelands and tribal identity. Maybe the vision of those times saw standing stones as a substitute body in which the souls of the dead were incorporated, a body built for eternity. Rocks are about as permanent as one can get in the physical world; our lifetime is the fraction of a blink of an eye in their time scale. One of the most potent magical acts is to carve and inscribe onto rock, for it makes the statement incredibly long lasting. One can see why the Masons are a secret fraternity – creating ideas with their carving of stone that they hoped would outlast generations.

In the late Neolithic/early Bronze Age, when the Kingston Russell Stone Circle was built, there was probably a similar idea. Stone circles will forever be an enigma. A people who had left the nomadic hunting life, to settle in communities around small farmsteads, erected them. Their tools were simple: antler picks, flint axes and, with the first usage of metal, bronze axes, spearheads and daggers. The late Neolithic merging into the early Bronze Age was a period of great change. The great long barrows, mass burial sites associated with the early Neolithic period, were ceremonially closed down and filled in with earth and the entrances were blocked with huge stones. Round barrows then took the place of long barrows and the early barrows, from around 2500 BC, contained inhumations accompanied by clay pots known as 'beakers'. The earliest beakers were found in Germany and it is possible that the closure of the long barrows was an indication that a new wave of immigration was occurring in Britain, and with these people came different ways of interring the dead. The long barrows contained the remains of those who were special to the indigenous people already settled in Britain – their chiefs, warriors and shamans. To close these places of ritual and otherworldliness, as the Bronze Age people did, was to contain and nullify access to the ancestors of the earlier people of these Isles.

Rocks were also used in the idea of making the cosmos manifest on earth. Attuning the stones with the constellations of stars and the planets signifies the concept 'as above, so below'. Kingston Russell Stone Circle is unusual in that all the stones are apparently fallen or possibly have been deliberately pushed over, maybe to mitigate the 'pagan' quality of the circle. It is said that one or more of the stones was still standing in the 19th century. Despite this, some people believe that the stones never were upright, and certainly, looking at what remains of the stones above ground, they appear to be unlike the monoliths that make up many circles, being in their natural state of rough sarsen boulders.

There is another ancient site in the area, an earlier Neolithic long barrow called the Grey Mare and Her Colts. This is a mainly collapsed structure, with only the large stones comprising the forecourt still standing.

A mile or so away, toward Hardy's Monument, is a natural landscape feature – the Valley of Stones. Here in a wide valley, set within the gentle rise of the hills, are drifts of sarsen stones. This area was probably an important site for our Neolithic and Bronze Age ancestors, who in all certainty used many of the stones for burial chambers and other ritual activities. It is managed by Natural England as a National Nature Reserve. Spring is a good time to visit this valley, strewn with clumps of bluebells and bright primroses. As summer arrives, the grasses and verbiage grow tall and start to partially obscure the hundreds of sarsen stones here, ranging from large to small, deposited in the last Ice Age. Similar to the area known as the Grey Wethers near Marlborough in Wiltshire, these stones are a rare natural anomaly. There are other groups of stones in the adjacent valley underneath Crow Hill but the larger amount is here.

The random deposits form no specific pattern except in one central area where the discerning eye can make out a rough circle of stones. It is unlikely that this is wholly natural, but whether this is the remains of a ceremonial stone circle or an enclosure or large burial cairn is difficult to prove. Ancient landscapes are hard to 'read' without appropriating modern conclusions.

BEAMINSTER
Buckham Down, Meerhay and Daniel's Knowle

OS maps: Explorer 117, or Landranger 193 and Landranger 194

Grid refs: Buckham Down car park ST484034, Meerhay Manor ST485026, Daniel's Knowle ST469005

Directions: For Buckham Down and Meerhay take the A3066 (Tunnel Road) from Beaminster towards Crewkerne. After approx. 1 mile and after passing through the tunnel, turn right towards Maiden Newton. After 1 mile turn right into Buckham Down car park and picnic site. The track for Meerhay Manor runs adjacent to the car park, leading steeply downhill. Various footpaths are found within the environs of the Manor, all of which lead into some wonderful countryside. The Wessex Ridgeway, Brit Valley Circular Walk, Monarch Way and Beaminster Ramblers' Millennium Trail all pass near here. For Daniel's Knowle take the B3163 west out of Beaminster, and opposite the school turn left to Stoke Abbott. After 600 m, park and walk the drive/bridleway to Knowle Farm. Daniel's Knowle is clearly visible approx. 200 m behind the farm cottages, but it is on private land so without permission it must be viewed from a distance.

Nearby refreshments: Beaminster

Sweet Be'mi'ster, that bist aboun'
By green an' woody hills al roun';
Wi' hedges, reachen up between
A thousan' viel's o' zummer green,
Where elems' lofty heads do drow
Ther shiades var hay-miakers below.
An' wilde hedge-flow'rs do charm th' souls
O' maidens in ther evening strolls.

William Barnes

Beaminster probably started as a settlement in the wooded valley of the meandering River Brit. A Roman road is less than a mile away and this road is constructed upon an older British one, which branched from the Wessex Ridgeway near Winyard's Gap and passed over Beaminster Down, where Bronze Age tumuli stand. After the Roman conquest there could have been a small Romano-British community in the river valley here. Certainly the town was occupied in Anglo-Saxon times, as the word *minster* is a sure indication of a Saxon ecclesiastical foundation. The full explanation of its name is *Bega's-minster* or church and in some ancient deeds the word is written *Bege-minster*. Bega or Bees was a saint, originally a holy woman from Ireland. In AD 650 she founded the monastery of St Bees near Copeland Forest in Cumberland. There can be no way of knowing how the pious St Bega became associated with Beaminster. She may not have necessarily founded or even contributed to the foundation of the original Saxon church, although it is possible. It is also possible that as the fame of her sanctity was known throughout most of England, some admirer might have dedicated the church to her.

This pretty town lies enfolded by hills and is situated on the edge of the Marshwood Vale. At one time factories manufacturing sailcloth and woollen articles provided employment, although the staple for the town was agriculture and associated trades. Famous Dorset Blue Vinny cheese used to be made here. Now all but one of the factories have long since disappeared and a large proportion of the town's residents are incomers who have retired to the area. Many pleasant buildings line the streets, but the three great fires of 1644, 1684 and 1781 destroyed most of the mediaeval buildings so that what remains is mostly 18th and 19th century. The church of St Mary escaped the blazes and the spectacular 16th century tower dominates the area.

Many places in West Dorset were affected by Monmouth's rebellion. Certain villages and towns held people who backed Monmouth, being sympathetic to the Protestant cause and affected by the charisma of the young Duke. One of these was James Daniel, a lawyer living in Beaminster. He joined the standard of Monmouth soon after the young Pretender landed at Lyme Regis in 1685, and was present at the decisive battle of Sedgemoor. He managed to escape from the field and reach Beaminster and his home. However, being a man of influence and property, a reward was soon offered for his capture and he realised, with the knowledge that the terrible Judge Jeffreys was holding sessions in nearby Dorchester, that he must flee. During a session of prayer prior to departure, he heard a voice, seemingly angelic, saying 'Flee to the West' and, heeding this, he went to Knowle, a mile or so west of the town. He hid himself under straw in a barn and prayed that he might be kept safe. Soon after, soldiers entered the building and eagerly thrust their swords into the straw, but they somehow missed finding Daniel and he avoided capture. He felt that he had been miraculously preserved by Providence, an act that made the old barn blessed. After 4 years, when the hounding of Monmouth's supporters had died down, he bought the

barn and an adjoining plot as a burial place for himself and his descendants. He lived until the ripe old age of 100. Many of his descendants lie buried here, in ground that was eventually consecrated in 1860. Known as Daniel's Plot or Daniel's Knowle, this historic family burial plot is surrounded by a thick hedge, with stone pillars standing either side of locked iron gates. A more detailed history and possibly access is available from the current owner Rupert Willoughby (www.rupertwilloughby.co.uk/daniels-knowle).

Northeast of Beaminster, running atop the hills that surround the town, is the Wessex Ridgeway. This prehistoric track, later enlarged and paved by the Romans, affords great views, and from Buckham Down over Beaminster is one of them. The diverse countryside and topography culminate in the luminosity of the sea, with hills, fields, woods, farms and town conjoining in a satisfying panorama. The car park and picnic area were formerly a refuse dump, and now some sculptures decorate the site.

The varied countryside around Beaminster is somehow a grand landscape on a small scale. Despite the humanising influence of the small farms, there is the feeling of something hidden and untamed. The town is neat enough but the land is not. When disparate elements in a landscape pull together to form a whole they are said to be the expression of the *genius loci*. What we see is in some way a product of our imagination – an emotional reaction, whether a feeling of awe or a sense of beauty. In Latin, *genius* means spirit and *loci* means 'of a place'. The *genius loci* therefore is the distinctive atmosphere and pervading spirit of a place. It can also be thought of as the guardian deity of an area. Although symbolism and sanctity are what *we* invest the landscape with through

imagination, the original integrity of an area is represented by the *genius loci*. To understand the real essence of the landscape we have to 'get out of the way' and let the place speak to us. Trees, stones, plants, mosses, insects, birds, animals – all these are part of the orchestra, the denizens of a particular environment. Appreciation of the landscape is not just a visual experience – there are sounds, such as bird song, wind rattling the branches of trees and buzzing insects, and smells, of flowers, wet grass and sea-salt spray, and sensations, such as the warm sun, caress of long grass and chill of rain. Elements of a place come to us via our senses but the truth of a place strikes deeper; it is more of an intuitive feeling, difficult to describe.

The 16th-century manor house and scattering of houses and cottages that comprise the hamlet of Meerhay used to have two archery butts during the time of Henry VIII. The landowners who live here seem to have come to an informal agreement that the wilder parts of the surrounding landscape will be left with a minimum of interference. This action preserves the wildwood and rough pastureland and provides a rare piece of countryside that illustrates the beauty of what might have been, of what we have lost throughout much of England. The scrubland, no good for farming and difficult to walk through, deemed as a useless pocket of land, is actually a valuable resource. Here is a breathing space for wildlife, a piece of ground exemplifying the symmetry of natural growth and decay.

In 2009 a Lithuanian man who was working on a farm near Meerhay Manor saw what he described as a wolf padding along the edge of a field. As wolves are still quite common in Lithuania, he thought nothing was untoward but mentioned the sighting to his employer as there could be a risk to the farm stock. Of course he was disbelieved, as the last wolf in Britain was killed in Scotland in the early 17th century. Yet the man was adamant, describing a large creature that was similar to an Alsatian dog, but bigger, leaner and with longer legs, an archetypal wolf in fact. There have been two other sightings of a wolf roughly 7 miles away on the lower slopes of Lewesdon Hill. A local farmer saw a wolf twice in his fields, as recounted below in the book by Merrily Harpur (*Roaring Dorset! Encounters with Big Cats*):

> *Lewesdon Hill – 29 August and October 2003. The* Bridport and Lyme Regis News *reported a sighting of a wolf: 'Pensioner Dudley Tolley, near Stoke Abbott, says he isn't crying wolf – he really did see one on Sunday! Mr Dudley Tolley of Stoke Knapp Farm, who has lived in the area all his life, said he was out checking his cattle in the early morning, about 6.15 a.m. He was going down the lane opposite his house, and saw it coming down the lane from Lewesdon Hill towards him. He saw it before it saw him. He said: "When it was 15 yards away from me I could see it was a wolf. It was dark grey, taller than a large Alsatian, with spindly legs – not as thick-set as an Alsatian. It looked at me as though it was thinking shall I go back or shall I go through the hedge? It was unhurried. Then it went through the hedge, and I went to the gate to see where it had gone but there was no sign of it. It was a beautiful animal in very good condition. I have never seen a wolf in the wild before." Mr Tolley said he contacted the police who did not seem interested and also DEFRA's animal health team. "I am hoping someone will arrange to capture it," he said. In October 2003 he saw it again from a hundred yards away, chasing sheep. "It went after them so slowly. Not darting about fast like a dog does. I have shot an Alsatian doing it, so I know the difference. When it saw me it went off fast."*

What is interesting is that there was not the wholesale carnage of livestock that would be expected if a wolf were at large. Sheep are the easiest of animals for a large predator to catch, yet no torn and bloodied carcases were found. There have been big cat sightings around this area too, glimpses of elusive cat-like animals that fail to fall into any definite physical category. Sometimes they are the size of panthers or leopards, sometimes the size of large dogs. Often they are black but occasionally brown or other colours. There are no firm conclusions as to whether these creatures actually physically exist or whether they are 'fae', otherworldly, part of that strange in-between place that implodes subtly upon our world in a way that defies rational explanation. Patrick Harpur, in his excellent book *Daimonic Reality*, presents a case for these creatures, which appear to have the quality of those beings known to a certain strand of ancient Greek philosophers as *daimons*. Daimons are somewhere between having a material physicality yet being also paradoxically immaterial. They are also shape-shifters, taking on appearances that suit the sensibility of those who perceive them. Illogical they may be, but their very illogicalness is part of the subtle truth that they are trying to present. Sightings of big cats and wolves suggest that a template still exists for those creatures and others now extinct that once roamed the ancient ice-scarred pristine fastnesses of Britain. They are still part of the inner landscape of these Isles, still existing faintly in the soul and in the land, like a memory that can never be totally extinguished.

BETTISCOMBE
Wishing Stone and Screaming Skull

OS maps: Explorer 116 or Landranger 193

Grid refs: Car park SY399999, Wishing Stone ST403005

Directions: Approx. 4 miles west of Broadwindsor on the B3164, just before Birdsmoorgate, turn south to Bettiscombe. Park in the village hall car park and take the footpath up the drive towards Bettiscombe Manor. Skirt around the west of the house and ascend Sliding Hill. Take the right fork in the path and approx. halfway up the hill the Wishing Stone can be seen about 50 m to your right (an elder tree grows quite near it). The stone is on private land and cannot be approached, but it is visible. The path continues up to the B3164, and a circular walk can be enjoyed by taking the left path at the top which leads back down to the original path just before the Manor.

Nearby refreshments: Shave Cross Inn, Shave Cross; Bottle Inn, Marshwood

Bettiscombe is a hamlet in the Marshwood Vale, near the highest hill in Dorset, Pilsdon Pen. Bettiscombe Manor is situated in a particularly beautiful position with a sheltered yet open outlook. The Manor is renowned for its screaming skull, reputed to scream if removed from the house. For years the skull was thought to be that of a Negro servant brought to Dorset from the West Indies by Azariah Pinney at the beginning of the 18th century. Because the Negro's request to be buried back in the West Indies on his death was ignored, his burial in the churchyard was followed by nightly screams and moans. After his body was brought into the manor house the noises ceased and for years the skull was thought to be his. In the 19th century a tenant living in the house threw the grisly relic into a pond, but after a while the unearthly moans eventually forced the tenant to restore the skull to its previous position.

In 1963 Michael Pinney, a descendant of Azariah, had the skull examined by a pathologist who asserted that it was that of a woman in her thirties dating from between 3000 and 4000 years ago. It was perhaps unearthed from the Iron Age temple site or a prehistoric barrow on nearby Pilsdon Pen, a legendary important druid site, a place of learning and teaching. Burials, where the head has been severed after death, have occasionally been found in barrows dating from the early Iron Age through to Romano-British and even Saxon times, possibly linked to the Celtic head cult. For the Celts, skulls were thought to have oracular properties, being a link with the gods and the soul. Maybe the Bettiscombe skull is a guardian spirit, screaming at any displacement.

The hill behind the Manor has the peculiar name of Sliding Hill. Once through the gate, one can see, on the right, a generally cleared area dominated

by a large stone. This is not the Wishing Stone but another recently discovered smaller stone. Not many natural sarsen stones are found in this area and it is difficult to ascertain if this stone is a natural anomaly or a feature of some human agency.

As the path ascends the steep slope, halfway up on the right can be seen a hillock with a few trees growing on it. Behind can be seen something large and grey, partially obscured by bracken. This object reveals itself as an enormous rock, camouflaged by fronds, flowers and grasses. This is the Wishing Stone. Wishes were made upon it on the summer solstice and the rock was reputed to roll downhill on the dawn of that day and drink from the stream, before returning back up the aptly named Sliding Hill. There is an attested sympathy between rocks and water, particularly rocks around a holy well. They seem to absorb the virtues of the spring they protect, so that the healing and oracular qualities of the well are extended into the surrounding area, enlarging the numinous quality of the shrine. Set at the head of a sheltering small valley, the Wishing Stone is backed by a tangled wildwood and the whole area seems untutored and sylvan. *Anima loci* is the 'soul' or innate essential spiritual nature

of a place manifested in physical form, and within the topography of this particular piece of land, the Wishing Stone is the keynote.

Rocks like this that are reputed in folklore to have independent life signify something beyond a literal interpretation of their movements. In the Cornish language, similar to the Welsh, a *carrek sans* means holy rock. A holy rock was one that was perceived to have magnetism, either naturally or which had been magnetised by the skills of certain people adept in the arts of energy transference, such as shamans or priests and priestesses of the old nature-based religion. Because rocks and stones hold energy, a magnetised rock is a receptacle of power and psychic forces that have an indefinite time scale. Standing stones contain this charged energy, as do some individual large rocks, such as Blackingstone Rock near Moretonhampstead and Arthur's Stone in North Wales. Certain rocks are naturally energised with a strong magnetic flow and examples can be found all over Britain and Ireland. Obvious contenders are some of the rocks that comprise the striking tors, the massive granite outcrops on the moors of Dartmoor and Bodmin, and those in the wildernesses of northern England. Granite is one of the oldest, hardest and most durable rocks and the indestructible quality of its makeup is reflected in Kes Tor on the edge of Dartmoor above Chagford.

The late seer, Robert Scrutton, known as 'the wizard of Dartmoor', used to say that Kes Tor was the central focus of pilgrimage and gathering in far-off times. It was (and maybe still is) a focal point for people who gather and conduct rites that would draw in the influences of the sun, moon and stars and make communion with beings whose existence is now mainly (but not completely) hidden from us. On the top of this enormous rock is a perfectly round rock basin, full of still water. Here could be seen in the dark of night the reflection of the moon's pale face shining as an oracle. Surrounding Kes Tor is a plethora of ancient sacred structures – the stone circle of Scorhill on a nearby hilltop and near the base of Kes Tor the prehistoric spirit paths, the stone rows too narrow for human feet to travel. The remains of burial chambers and a large standing stone complete the complement of structures that help harness and define the spiritual landscape.

The rock known as 'The Stone of Scone', placed under the Coronation throne in Westminster Abbey, is a good example of a rock seen to contain power and has an interesting history. Legend ascribes it to being one of the Four Treasures of the Tuatha de Danaan, a mysterious early people linked with Ireland. They brought the stone from an island in the Atlantic Ocean called Falias, one of a group of four. The rock was known as the Stone of Destiny and has been identified as the stone mentioned in the *Old Testament* (*Genesis* xxviii, 18–22) brought by the prophet Jeremiah to Ireland. Jeremiah's tomb is said to be at Loch Erne. In AD 502 the stone was taken to Scotland by King Fergus and he and his successors, numbering 34 in all, were crowned on it. In 1296 Edward I, realising the history and power of this stone, had it taken to Westminster and the present Coronation chair made for it. It would be interesting to see what happens if the stone were ever returned to Scotland or indeed Ireland.

Dowsers, sharing a kinship of sensitivity with the shaman, often pick up a magnetic field around rocks and there is a sort of alchemy in certain landscapes comprised of the combinations and components of the different rocks in an area. Sometimes this is a beneficial mix, sometimes less human-friendly and more private, referring to the integrity of some areas that benefit without intrusion. There are certain places where we are not welcome, where wildness should be left to brood without the merry clamour of human voices.

There was a time when certain stones seemed alive and magic and mystery animated the countryside, giving vibrancy to the workaday world. So-called pagan nonsense plays little part in our lives today, and with it a certain respect has gone. We have lost so many of our ancient standing stones, circles and other artefacts from the past, grubbed up for building or destroyed because they got in the way of the tractor and plough. They are seen as dead and inanimate, but that is not quite true. When we hold things in reverence, we are not necessarily being held in thraldom by so-called quaint custom and superstition. We are more likely recognising the special and primal interrelatedness between the environment and ourselves. If we defy logic and opt for a more expanded view of what science tells us is 'true', we move into an imaginative realm, which propels us to go further and engenders an expansion of consciousness. What constitutes 'meaning' is given a more infinite possibility.

BROADWINDSOR
Black Dogs

OS maps: Explorer 116 or Landranger 193

Grid refs: Church parking ST437026, Pond ST448028

Directions: From the Broadwindsor one-way system, head northeast on the B3164 towards Mosterton. Almost immediately, you pass the church on your left (where you may wish to park). Common Water Lane is on the opposite side of the road, and parking space is extremely limited along the lane. The first half mile of the lane is tarmac road and you can turn your car where the tarmac ends and walk to view the pond, but from there it becomes a track which is often rather muddy.

Nearby refreshments: Broadwindsor

Common Water Lane is part of the Wessex Ridgeway, one of the best-known ancient tracks in England. This track, Neolithic in all certainty, is an upland route through some of the southern counties of England, ending on the Dorset/Devon coast at Lyme Regis. The part of the track known as Common Water Lane travels through Broadwindsor, continuing towards Beaminster and beyond. It is a lovely old lane, during the day at least, affording beautiful views of hills and unimproved pastureland.

Following the directions above, a short diversion is afforded after a couple of hundred yards by a footpath on the left, which passes a large duck pond. This body of water is private, but the path offers a good view of the pond, which is a lovely secluded place to gaze at for a while. Retracing one's steps back to the lane, there is an exhilarating feeling of openness to this part of the track. The

fields on either side are ancient pastureland, and beyond can be seen wooded Lewesdon Hill, the flat top of Waddon Hill, and Gerrards Hill, with its crown of beech and Scots pine. A dreamy diverse landscape starts to emerge, for on the other side of the track the fields roll to the borders of Somerset and distant Blackdown Hills.

Progressing up the lane, the journey starts to feel, subtly, more eldritch. The crows caw with rough-edged hoarseness and wheel their black jaggedness against the sky. As the track dips and gently rises, the landscape develops a wilder feel, with patches of woodland, tree-tangled and unkempt. It is not surprising that the ghostly shaggy Black Dog, a Girt Dog, also pants and grizzles this way. Black Dogs, spirit creatures, omens of death and change, are found in folk-legend and actually sighted all over Britain. They are called by different names – the Welsh *Gwiyllgi*, the Highland *Cu Sith* and *Black Shuck* of East Anglia and Norfolk.

Ancient track-ways are a favourite haunt of these strange beings and this area is no exception. Local folklore links Common Water Lane with the Black Dog and there have been sightings recently, on the continuation of the lane on the west side of Broadwindsor, where it becomes Grange Lane and thence on in the direction of Burstock, beyond which it is named Park Water Lane. In the summer of 2009, as dusk was settling in, a local man, Neil Judd, saw a huge black dog walking away up the hill out of Broadwindsor by the old tollhouse and lane that leads to Hursey. He thought the dog unusually large, 'the size of a

Painting 2: Out of the misty shrouded shadows pads the Black Dog,
beast of folklore and legend.

calf and heavy-set with a large head, like a mastiff', and his initial concern was for his dog, a Golden Retriever. He thought that a huge strange dog wandering around loose could be a danger for other animals too.

Neil then had another sighting later that summer which was far more perturbing. It was dusk and he was cycling along Grange Lane, close to his first encounter. At the beginning of the lane, he saw the huge dog again, at the far end of a field. 'The dog saw me and started to run across the field towards me. I was really concerned for my own safety, so I started peddling fast towards Burstock, which was downhill. I cycled like a man possessed, worried that the dog would cut across the field and turn up in front of me, but it didn't appear, which was a relief.' The same year, Neil was driving on the B3164 towards Mosterton between the hours of 10 and 11 pm. A mile or so from Broadwindsor, at the beginning of Potwell Covert, he saw the dog again, standing in a gateway. 'I went on about a hundred yards, hesitated and then reversed back, but it had gone.' Neil had a fourth sighting that year whilst on the early morning London train from Crewkerne. A couple of miles out of the station, between Misterton and North Perrott, he saw the creature running across a field. It is possible that this Black Dog, haunting a wide area around Broadwindsor, was the inspiration for *The Hound of the Baskervilles* by Sir Arthur Conan Doyle. He stayed in nearby Beaminster in the 1920s and one night heard the eerie howling of a dog. It is said that these howls gave him the idea for the story.

Another tale of the Black Dog is even more sinister. Not many years ago, two young women were walking on a winter evening on Burton Bradstock cliff. One of the women was a *feng-shui* practitioner and the two had apparently just performed a 'cleansing' of the energies at a nearby site. As they strolled along the cliff path, slowly a wind started to whip up and then they saw in an adjoining field a black shape running fast towards them. As it got nearer, they could see that it was as big as a calf and had eyes the size of saucers, a classic 'Black Dog'. The wind now threatened to blow them off the cliff and the dog was approaching fast … and then it disappeared. Slowly the wind subsided, leaving the women shaken. These dogs have a guardianship quality and perhaps the women had been well meaning but had upset the balance of some powerful and fairy place.

Maybe some of our ancient lanes are also spirit ways, for those other than human. Maybe things pass, moving sometimes fast, sometimes slow, entities enshrined in legend and imagination yet sometimes seeming to have physical life. Events happen that shake our preconceptions of normal life and these events can open doorways into a different sort of reality, a reality over which we have little control. This could be considered an exciting prospect, offering new horizons and an expansion of our somewhat curtailed view of what is 'real' and what is not.

CHIDEOCK
Martyrs' Church and Castle Ruins

OS maps: Explorer 116 or Landranger 193

Grid refs: Whalebone arch SY421933, Church SY419935, Castle ruins and cross SY424931

Directions: From the A35 in Chideock, turn north down the lane alongside St Giles' Church, towards North Chideock. Approx. ¼ mile down this lane on the right is a whalebone arch over a gate. A little further on there is a small car park on the right for the church and museum. For the castle ruins you can take a circular walk behind Chideock Manor and Hell Lane. However, the shortest walking route is to park near Chideock village store, walk approx. 100 m east along the A35, then north up Ruins Lane. The castle remains are in the first field through the gate, marked by a large cross.

Nearby refreshments: George Inn and Village Store, Chideock; Seatown and Morecombelake

The origin of the name Chideock was probably the Old English word *Coediog*, which means woody. A small Roman settlement developed by the ford, where the Roman road crossed the River Winniford. Over the centuries there was a Saxon community here and later a Norman one. During the latter period, Chideock was in the hands of the de Mandervilles. In 1217, Geoffrey de Manderville granted the manor to Sir Thomas le Brithun. Three generations later, 'le Brithun' was changed to 'de Chideock'. The original manor house was fortified and a Royal licence obtained to transform the building into a castle.

Chideock is about a mile from the sea and dissected by the busy A35 trunk road. On one side is the way to the coast and the hamlet of Seatown. On the other is a lane leading to North Chideock. On the corner of this lane is the parish church of St Giles. Founded in the 13th century, on possible Saxon foundations, the church stands as a generic Gothic Victorian building, clamped on to a medieval core.

Aside the road to North Chideock is a strange whalebone arch over a small gate. The whalebone dates from 1880 when a whale was stranded on the beach. Further on is the Church of Our Lady Queen of Martyrs and St Ignatius. Prior to this church being built, Catholics in the area said Mass in Chideock Castle. Chideock Castle was founded in 1380 on land ceded by Edward II to Sir John de Chideock and the building was finished by his son in 1387. In Tudor times the castle and lands passed through marriage to Katherine Arundell. The staunchly Catholic Arundell family held these until the mid-17th century, the castle always being a Catholic stronghold. The family were fiercely Royalist during

Painting 3: The strange whale-bone arch spreading over a gateway
that leads into the gardens of the manor.

the Civil War and they eventually lost their estate. The Parliamentarian General Fairfax finally took the castle in 1645 and, with assistance of the Governor of Lyme Regis, the building was almost totally destroyed. What was left of the ruins was taken for building material and eventually only a gatehouse remained, standing until 1741. Like many ruins, Chideock Castle has acquired legends, including one of a mysterious golden table allegedly used by monks and still hidden somewhere in the ruins. Only banks and moat ditches now remain. The large Dorset-oak cross was erected in 1951 by Lt Col Humphrey Weld.

When the castle fell in 1645 the Catholics had to worship in any nook and cranny they could find. They were eventually covertly allowed to use the barn attached to a farmhouse known as Dame Hallett's, where they worshipped discretely for nearly 170 years. The estate of Chideock was returned to the Arundells after the Reformation, but they no longer lived in the area. A relation, Thomas Weld of Lulworth, bought the estate in 1802 for his son Humphrey. In 1805, Humphrey built a chapel in the old barn. In 1872 his son Charles Weld

Photo courtesy of John Steinmann

built a church on the site of this earlier chapel. Charles succeeded Humphrey in 1852 and wanted to convert his father's modest building into something much more ornate. Influenced by his tours to Europe, particularly Italy, he built the new church in a richly Romanesque style.

He left some of the older chapel intact, which now forms part of the priest's sacristy. Inside this room is part of the earlier chapel which reveals highly decorated walls and ceiling. A small staircase at the back of the room leads to the original place of worship in the 17th century, the loft in the barn. Here can be seen the old walls complete with faded paintings of great complexity and

age. The sacristy is open to visitors on special occasions or by arrangement. There is also an intriguing museum, approached through the church. On one of the walls of the sacristy is a powerful painting of the Chideock Martyrs by renowned local artist Francis H. Newbery, dating from 1929. The story of the martyrs is one of tragic barbarism. In 1570 Pope Pius V decreed that Elizabeth I should be excommunicated and that no Roman Catholic should recognise her legitimacy to rule. In anger she declared it treasonable for any Roman Catholic priest to live and serve in England and for all Roman Catholics to be regarded as potentially treasonable. This continued her father's slow but sure persecution of anyone who adhered to the Roman Catholic faith. Chideock has seven Catholic martyrs who suffered the traitor's fate, a cruel death of hanging, drawing and quartering. Thomas Pilchard, chaplain of the Arundell family, was the first to be condemned in 1587. Together with his companion William Pike, he was executed at Dorchester. In 1594, John Cornelius, chaplain to Lady Arundell, was betrayed, along with three other men, John Carey, Patrick Salmon and Thomas Bosgrove. It seems rather unlucky to be a chaplain to the Arundells, for in 1642 another chaplain, Hugh Green, was discovered on Lyme Cobb about to take a boat to France, and was summarily executed. John Jessop, known as the eighth martyr, died in Dorchester gaol.

This church remembers them, and portraits of the martyrs painted by various members of the Weld family are displayed along the nave. Their faces loom accusingly through the dim light. There is said to be a curse on the land around Chideock due to the persecution and barbarity afforded to the Chideock Martyrs. The executioner and most of the jury, sheriff and gaoler died soon after the martyrs' executions and a plague struck Dorchester. There was a belief that those who took land from Catholics suffered a curse that made their land poisoned, particularly around Whitchurch Canonicorum. There have been many accidents. A man digging a well died from fumes that were subtly issuing from the site. Another man was electrocuted when he inadvertently touched the pylons that loomed above him. It seems a sad history has left a taint on the area, but the human spirit is resolute and strong. This Roman Catholic church stands as a memorial to those who died for their beliefs but is also much more than that. The inspirational beauty and artistry that it contains show how a strong spiritual faith can rise above dark injustices.

CHIDEOCK
The Witches of Langdon Hill

OS maps: Explorer 116 or Landranger 193

Grid ref: National Trust Golden Cap car park SY413931

Directions: There is no sign, but approx. ½ a mile west out of Chideock, at the top of the hill, turn left into Muddyford Lane just before the dual carriageway begins. Almost immediately, turn left into Langdon Lane, a surprisingly rough track to the National Trust's pay & display car park. There is a 'natural' play trail here for children and a 1-mile accessible path circumnavigates Langdon Hill. There are numerous detour options including Golden Cap, Stonebarrow Hill and the SWCP.

Nearby refreshments: Morecombelake, Chideock and Seatown

Langdon Hill is a long, wooded hill rising above Chideock. The centre of the hill is Forestry Commission land, planted with firs, with the banks of the hill growing a fecund variety of trees such as oak, Scots pine, hawthorn and elder, these native trees adding variety to the monotony of the firs. There are lovely vistas from every part of the hill. In the east can be seen Thorncombe Hill above Eype, crowned with a tumulus. To the south is the sea and dramatic eminence of Golden Cap, the highest cliff on the south coast. To the west the coast curves around to Charmouth and Lyme Regis, bordered by Stonebarrow Hill, with its myriad hidden smugglers' paths. Northwest are the Iron Age hillforts of Coney's Castle, Lambert's Castle and Pilsdon Pen.

As one follows the path circumnavigating the hill, an old track is seen leading west down to the ruins of St Gabriel's Church, a church that served the fishing community of Stanton St Gabriel, now almost disappeared. Just a few holiday

cottages are left, vestiges of an old way of life. Fishing would be harder now because the path down to the beach has fallen away over the years. The land along this coast is famously unstable. Another old track leads down from the other side of the hill to Seatown, a coastal hamlet a mile from Chideock. This track has an eerie history, for it is reputed to be the route of an otherworldly Black Dog. West Dorset has numerous tales of such creatures, often seen near or on ancient roads.

Chideock has another mysterious attribute in that it was known to have possessed an ancient coven of hereditary witches and it is possible the descendants of this coven are still working here on the hill. Langdon Hill has a powerful presence, difficult to describe but palpable. Altars have been found in hidden-away locations. They are not obvious, there are just a few subtle clues, such as in the centre of a circle of trees the burnt-out remains of a small fire or perhaps an arrangement of twigs and foliage that seems the result of human artifice rather than the random design of nature.

In olden times witches were viewed with both reverence and suspicion. Many were more accurately wise women or herbalists than bona fide witches in the modern sense of the word. Most villages had someone who dispensed herbs and potions to the sick and was able to use 'vision' to prophesy the future. These people performed a service to the community and they were normally respected. But if animals sickened or someone was taken ill, there was always the risk that the village 'wise woman' or 'cunning man' would be accused of 'overlooking' people or animals, an accusation sometimes resulting in an attack.

Witchcraft has been with us for a long time. In mediaeval times, witches were thought to have gained their powers by having made a pact with the Devil. They were therefore regarded as heretics, renouncing God. The main agency behind this accusation was the Dominican Order within the Roman Catholic Church, which produced the *Malleus Maleficarum* of 1486. This was conjoined with an earlier Papal Bull of 1484, issued by Pope Innocent VIII. The origins of this particular notion of witchcraft probably came from a reaction to a proliferation of so-called heretical factions within Catholicism, such as the Cathars. The influence of this edict, combined with the belief that a witch could do harm to others, was responsible for bringing in the first Act of Parliament in 1542 which made witchcraft a statutory offence. This was followed by others and culminated in the final witchcraft statute of 1604, the most severe. This remained law until 1736, after which witchcraft was no longer a statutory offence. For centuries witches and so-called witches remained very vulnerable. There was a notion that witches bore a mark on their body that showed their profession, and anyone who had an unusual mole or blemish was at risk. Familiars, an imp or devil in the shape of an animal or insect, were also said to attend witches, and old reclusive villagers with their pet cat or dog could occasionally lose both their pet and their life.

That there were instances of malefic magic is beyond doubt. Cursing tablets, effigies stuck with pins, and magical formulae of all types have survived as proof that there were those who wished harm on others. Sometimes this might have been a last resort, seen as a justifiable way of protection against assault or wrongdoing. It was also widely thought that lack of charity or meanness to some old woman could result in misfortune – the milk going sour, sickness, animals falling lame. In an odd sort of way witch beliefs helped strengthen the moral code of kindness and charity because the fear of retaliation brought the realisation that if the strange old woman down the road were decently treated, she would not be inclined to hurt you.

The more spiritual way of understanding witches and shamans in a modern context is as people who see the natural world as alive with a mysterious numinous life and who celebrate the tides of the year and the tides within human life – birth, partnership and death. Witchcraft is now practised as a mystery religion with pagan overtones. A goddess and god are worshipped – the Mother Goddess, who gave birth to the world, and her consort, the Horned God, who made that birth possible. Much of this is influenced by the work of anthropologist Dr Margaret Murray in her two widely read books, *The Witch-Cult in Western Europe* (1921) and *The God of the Witches* (1931). She postulated that witchcraft was the 'old religion', an ancient pagan fertility cult that had always had a wide following. She also showed that there was a universal aspect to the various types of witchcraft still existing throughout the world, and her work revived a public interest in the Craft.

It took Gerald Gardner in the 1950s to open the door to a more in-depth view of the subject. Gardner claimed to have been initiated by a hereditary witch who was part of a coven in the New Forest and he felt that he spoke from experience, from an insider's viewpoint. He stated that witchcraft had gone underground and had never been totally obliterated by the ferocious persecutions that had continued over the years, reaching their venomous peak in the 16th and 17th centuries. Gardner's work in uncovering the various strands that make up the Craft and his publishing of various rites gained him followers. He formed a coven and started a form of witchcraft that became known as 'Gardnerian'. Many of his ideas were triggered by other magical organisations, such as the Golden Dawn, which were flourishing at the time. The Hermetic Order of the Golden Dawn, founded in 1888, incorporated Masonic, Celtic, Egyptian and Hermetic beliefs into a system of ritual magic. The Order attracted some of the luminaries of the day, including the Irish poet W.B. Yeats, actress Florence Farr and the infamous Aleister Crowley, who went on to found his own magical order.

Once Gardner started the ball rolling, modern witchcraft started to quickly gain momentum. Other people came to the forefront, such as Alex Saunders, Janet and Stewart Farrar, Dolores Ashcroft-Nowicki and Ralph Harvey. Saunders in particular became notorious for initiating large numbers of young people, some of whom succumbed to psychological problems afterwards because they had been insufficiently prepared beforehand. He developed a synchronic style of witchcraft known as Alexandrian, utilising aspects of ritual magic to a deeper degree than Gardner. With the addition of his own charismatic showmanship and a glamorous wife and magical partner, Maxine, his style of witchcraft developed a large following.

Present-day 'Traditionals' are a secretive group whose members are gathered from local rural communities and who work within what they consider to be their own native locale. Different from Alexandrian and Gardnerian groups but with a broad affiliation if not total similarity to hereditary witches, Traditional witches have as their main basis communication with the ancestral land and through that a link, an unbroken chain to the peoples of the distant past. Today witchcraft has a huge number of adherents all over the Western world. Appealing to those who want a nature-based religion with strong links to the feminine principle and to people who have become disaffected with Christianity and the church, the Wiccan creed has provided an outlet for people who want to express their spirituality in a way that incorporates both active worship and recognition of a goddess and god. This is combined with participation in an ancient indigenous knowledge that offers a deepened understanding of the natural world. Wiccans see the divine as an energy that permeates all living things. The material world, though different in substance from spirit, is realised as another expression of divine vitality.

Finally, we end with the old belief that a witch could take the form of a hare, cavorting on the hills in the dead of night under the pale unearthly light of the moon. Only a silver bullet would bring her down. John Symonds Udal in his book *Dorsetshire Folk-Lore* quotes a letter he received in 1893 from a vicar from

Cambridge. He recounts that a labourer from the Isle of Purbeck on his way home from work noticed yet again a hare that he kept encountering in the dim evening light near a stile. He was advised by a friend to put a silver sixpence in a gun and have a shot at the hare. He borrowed a gun and next time he saw the hare took a shot. As it limped away, he threw his sickle at it, which struck the hare but it still evaded capture. On his arrival home, a neighbour rushed in and said that 'Old Nanny's a-dying and wants to see 'ee. She's got a cut all across her back as if someone had cut it with a reaping hook!' Many rural people still refuse to eat hares because of their magical associations.

The Old Witch-Hare by Walter de la Mare

In the black furror of a field
I saw an old witch-hare this night;
And she cocked a lissom ear,
And she eyed the moon so bright,
And she nibbled of the green,
And I whispered 'Whsst! Witch-hare!'
Away like a ghostie o'er the field
She fled, and left the moonlight there.

CONEY'S CASTLE
A Haunted Hillfort

OS maps: Explorer 116 or Landranger 193

Grid ref: National Trust car park SY372978

Directions: From Hunters Lodge Inn, just east of Axminster on the A35 at Raymond's Hill, take the B3165 north to Crewkerne. After approx. 3 miles, and before Lambert's Castle, turn right to Fishponds. After ½ mile there is a confusing mix of road junctions, but ignore the signs for Marshwood, Fishpond Bottom and Whitchurch and continue on under the power cables towards Wootton Fitzpaine. Coney's Castle car park is just ¼ mile on the left.

Nearby refreshments: Bottle Inn, Marshwood; Five Bells Inn, Whitchurch Canonicorum

Coney's Castle is an Iron Age hillfort just south of the larger and better known Lambert's Castle. Thought to date from 500 BC, it is the smallest hillfort in the area and one of the most intriguing. A lane now runs through the middle, but the few vehicles that use this route do not spoil the ambiance of this ancient and historic place.

The name Coney's Castle is a corruption of King's Castle. Many people have thought the name means 'fortified place frequented by coneys (rabbits)', but history favours the royal connection. This hillfort has a double bank and ditch and was built by the local Durotriges tribe as a defence against the neighbouring Dumnonii. It was used as a hillfort for hundreds of years and in the early 9th

century Saxon King Egbert, after whom the castle was probably named, using the fort as his base, drove away a large band of marauding Danes who had been ravaging the area.

In comparison with Pilsdon Pen, Lewesdon Hill and Lambert's Castle, Coney's Castle displays less immediately obvious charms. Yet the view to the southwest, taking in the wooded rolling sweep of the Dorset/Devon border and the glimmering coast at Charmouth, is full of beauty. This part of the hillfort dramatically drops away into the valley, providing a natural defence. The slopes are covered with ancient woodland, inaccessible and growing freely. The steep hillside in the west was probably instrumental in the fort being built on this particular hill. There is a small car park beside the fort and from here tracks follow the banks and ditches of the earthwork. These shaded paths that trace the contours of the hill are full of wild flowers at certain times of the year.

During Celtic times, hillforts were not only places of warfare but also fortified settlements where people lived all year round, growing simple crops in the small fields they created around the base of the fort and raising a few domestic animals – sheep, similar to the hardy Soay sheep, a small breed of cattle, something like the little black Dexter cow, and pigs developed from the wild boar. Their wheat crop would have been of the simple low-gluten type known as spelt and a type of oat was grown. Nuts, berries, tubers and various leafy plants were all wild-sourced for additional food.

Historical record associates Coney's Castle with the aforementioned Anglo-Saxon King Egbert and his battle with the Danes. The earlier occupations of the fort leave no record apart from the fortifications; the banks and ditches are just the remnants of a structure that lasted for nearly a thousand years. There have been few archaeological discoveries and little to physically show for the waves of successive peoples who have lived here.

Sometimes though there is an atmosphere left in certain places, particularly those associated with the unforgiving aspects of life, such as warfare. There are those who have visited and felt unsettling sensations around a certain area of Coney's Castle. Across the fort, diagonally from the car park, near the start of Long Lane where there is a meeting of two tracks, is an area that feels unnerving to some people. In fact a few years ago a psychic research group was asked to visit this spot. Unease spread to some of the members and an odd stillness and chill was also noticed, but there was no definite sighting of anything, nor any sound or strange smell. Whether this was a site of death associated with the fort's history as a defensive structure or whether a murder took place here in more recent times, the mystery of the unsettling atmosphere remains.

Sometimes there are natural 'cold spots' in the landscape that have nothing to do with human agency, but more with areas that are said to be 'goblin haunted'. There are different explanations for this type of phenomenon. Dowsers describe these places as the recipients of negative energy nodes, where there is stagnation in the natural flow of energies that course through the earth,

Painting 4: Part of the ancient woodland on the southwest flanks of Coney's Castle. This part of the hillfort, with its primeval wood and steep slopes, feels like a landscape that has had little intrusion to disturb it.

causing them to pool and collect in certain sites, thereby creating an area that emanates a subtle sense of decay and heaviness. Then there is a quite literal explanation – the area *is* goblin haunted and human egress is resented. The different strata that make up the companies of fairies comprise both the tricky and the more benevolent; goblins have always been thought of as malevolent beings. There was a literal belief in fairies within the country community up until the 19th century. The age of mechanisation eroded the links with both the natural and supernatural worlds and the world of the 'fae' slowly faded from people's consciousness. Fairies are thought to exist by many people all over the world. It is the imaginative faculty of our minds that gives them shape and if there is no belief in them there is also no comprehension of their existence. There is an old saying that the fairies disappeared because no one believed in them anymore, and that could be true. One could say that 'the fair folk' haven't totally disappeared, just disappeared for us.

It is worth thoroughly exploring this fort, taking a walk along the path on the banks and crossing the lane to explore the small meadows on the edge of the steeply wooded hillside. A real bonus is the view that takes in a variety of scenery, all of it lovely. To the west is the hamlet of Fishponds edging towards Monkton Wyld and wooded Raymond's Hill. Fishponds is evocatively named, with the suggestion that ponds were here at one time, either as a natural result of the activity of springs or artificially built, as were many around mediaeval priories and abbeys, although no sign of these can be seen here now. These ponds were dug to keep carp, regarded as an important food item.

Gazing towards Devon, with the landscape reaching out to the Blackdown Hills in the distance, it is interesting to note the difference between the two counties, for from this view the Devon hills are long and wooded and less individual than those of West Dorset. To the south is the gleam of the sea and the open gorse-studded ground of Stonebarrow Hill. Lyme Bay unfolds into the horizon, a horizon that at some past time would have been intermittently dotted with the warrior longboats of the Vikings and Danes coming to berth on the beach at Charmouth. Once they landed, coming in by moonlight, silently, stealthily, bringing with them the battle ethos of the wild cruel gods they worshipped, they would lay siege to the area. As ferocious warriors they took by force the lives of the people and the land, despoiling what they could not use and roughly taking what they wanted. Coney's Castle was a watch point for this ingress and from here would be sent the native warriors to rout the invaders. Sometimes battles were won, sometimes lost, all part of the chequered history of invasions that make up the story of Britain. Now the view to the sea is one of peace and beauty and the far-off fears remain as folk tales.

CORSCOMBE
The Devil's Chair and a Haunting Lane

OS maps: Explorer Map 117 or Landranger 194

Grid refs: Parking ST517055, Corscombe stones ST514048, Common Lane (start) ST517056

Directions: Between Maiden Newton and Beaminster on the A356, turn to Corscombe at Corscombe Cross. After approx. 1 mile, turn right into the main part of the village. The start of Common Lane is approx. 300 m on your left, near Bankside, but this can be explored later. Instead, continue on a short way and park in or near to Barrow Lane, which is on your right. At the end of the Lane take the footpath uphill and after approx. 250 m go through the gate on your left. Follow the often overgrown path to the right and down, through a clearing, to a small field containing the Corscombe stones.

Nearby refreshments: Fox Inn, Corscombe

Corscombe is a sprawling village halfway down a hill. Neolithic and Roman remains have been found, implying that there has been a settlement here since earliest times. The name is thought to have come from the Old English *Cors Weg Cumb*, which means 'valley of the road in the pass'. Up to the mid-20th century the village was self-sufficient, as so many were at that time, with shops, a school and pub. There was a tailor, butcher, baker and cobbler. A mill ground the grain and farms produced meat, milk, butter and eggs (free-range eggs are still supplied by a couple of farms, as is lamb and pork). People toiled on the land or for the tannery, brick-kiln, lime-kiln and chalk pit, all of which provided work. Many craftsmen plied their trade, such as the blacksmith and the Sartin brothers, one of whom was a hurdle-maker and thatcher and the other a wheelwright. Today the family name still has presence in the songs of Bonny Sartin, a stalwart of the folk group 'The Yetties'.

Another interesting character with connections with Corscombe is Thomas Hollis (1720–74). Hollis was a gentleman scholar and libertarian philosopher who had been left 700 acres by his uncle, a generous man who was also the principal benefactor of the famous American university Harvard. Thomas Hollis retained the family link with Harvard, endowing the university with many volumes of priceless books. He was a disciplined man, rejecting alcohol, milk, sugar and butter, mainly for reasons of health as he had a fear of dying a lingering death because of some illness. His fears proved unfounded as he dropped dead in one of his fields. He is secretly buried in another, along with his horse. Which field contains his remains is open to conjecture. He lived at Urless Farm in Corscombe but also had connections with Harvard Farm near Halstock, so either area has a legitimate claim. His memory is carried in the farms and fields he named— Liberty Farm, Massy Field (Massachusetts), Toleration and Republic.

Following the directions above will bring you to something completely unexpected, a group of huge sarsen stones. These are Corscombe's secret stones, unmarked on the map and for the most part unrecorded. They are probably the remains of a little-known chambered long barrow, similar to the Grey Mare and Her Colts above Abbotsbury. The Corscombe stones comprise three groups of large stones, with other stones scattered around the edges of the field. The principal group of three is probably the remains of a crescent forecourt. One stone looks like a crude chair and in the past many prehistoric sites, with their links with paganism and pre-Christian activity, were attributed to the Devil's work, hence the name of this stone, 'the Devil's Chair'.

Long barrows were built roughly between 4000 and 2500 BC. They were tombs and centres of religious activity, based around a cult of ancestors and the dead. Who knows how these early people viewed death? The bones found in long barrows were mainly skulls and long bones, implying that they were interred after exposure elsewhere. It is possible that these remains provided a link to highly valued members of the community and were used in an oracular way. Long barrows were more places of respect than fear, providing stability and reassurance to the people who honoured them. The relics they contained, combined with their impressive presence, created an edifice that was an important cohesive element in the society of the time.

Sometimes there is a small offering of flowers here, particularly in spring when primroses fill this secluded spot with little dabs of pale yellow. At Halloween there have been candles lit by the stones in a sense of communion with the past. During daylight the stones have the air of some peaceful soliloquy, but when night falls they can assume the stance of watchers, inhuman and ageless.

Barrow Lane leads to the stones and is an old route. Underfoot can be seen half-hidden cobblestones and older, rougher stones used for paving. This ancient

track would appear to be a continuation of Common Lane (see the directions), which leads to Halstock and ends by the site of a Roman villa. Common Lane starts innocently enough, passing a farm and stables and meandering down an incline bordered by meadows and copses. Bear left towards the slopes of Wood Fold Hill and traverse upwards, towards trees meeting overhead to form a tunnel, getting darker, deeper, silent and still.

Some locals think this part of the lane is haunted, but no one can say by what, it is just a 'feeling', a slight unease. Our history has lain across the landscape over thousands of years. The imprints are everywhere. Folk memory has nearly forgotten the deeds that fuelled story and legend and the modern rational mind depopulates the countryside of its spirits and fairies. So who can now say anything on why places feel 'strange' or what the real beliefs were of the people who honoured their dead with the long barrows?

Painting 5: The enigmatic Corscombe stones, brooding quietly in an undisturbed green and pastoral valley.

CORSCOMBE
Bracketts Coppice

OS maps: Explorer 117 or Landranger 194

Grid refs: Dorset Wildlife Trust car parks and information boards at ST514068 and ST514074

Directions: Between Maiden Newton and Beaminster on the A356, turn to Corscombe at Corscombe Cross. After skirting the western edge of Corscombe continue northwest towards Higher Halstock Leigh. Approx. 1 mile out of Corscombe, the road turns sharply left, and the first parking area is approx. 150 m on the right, behind a metal gate.

Nearby refreshments: Village store, Halstock; Winyards Gap Inn, Chedington; Fox Inn, Corscombe

Bracketts Coppice is a lovely area of unspoilt land consisting mostly of woods and small fields that undulate down to a tree-strewn valley and a rocky stream where otters have been seen. Wildlife thrives here and there are hare, deer, dormice, bats, including the rare Bechstein's bat, and a varied selection of birds, such as Grey Wagtails, Kingfishers and Nuthatches. Silver-Washed and Marsh Fritillaries are amongst the butterflies found fluttering over the swathes of wild flowers. In early summer the fields are awash with orchids and in autumn many edible fungi can be found. Some of the fields are cut for hay and some grazed by cattle – sensitive ways of unobtrusive management, which encourage wildflowers and a diversity of grasses.

What this reserve gives is an intimate link with old-fashioned pastures and ancient woodland. There is a real sense of peace here and the realisation that any human influence is gentle and undemanding. Nature is benign when not threatened by unfeeling intrusion and, when benign, secrets are revealed which in other circumstances could remain hidden.

One of the secrets is the giant copper-coloured hare. A woman walking her dog through the ancient meadows and enjoying the rich autumn colours of a late October was startled by what she thought was a small deer, a Muntjac perhaps, rising up at the edge of the woodland. But no Muntjac are found in the Coppice and the woman realised that what she was seeing was an extremely large hare. An employee of the reserve has also seen this animal, as have I. As I was walking in meadows on the edge of the woods, I saw something reddish hiding in the grasses, which on my approach loped off. It was a hare at least twice the size of a usual hare, with gleaming fur that was of a chestnut-orange colour rather than the more subdued hue of the regular brown hare.

The hare has been thought of as a lunar magical creature and messenger of the spirit world by many different cultures. Capable of shape-shifting and linked with witchcraft, in that folklore has witches changing into hares, it has also been seen as a fertility symbol linked with the Celtic goddess of spring and dawn, Eostre. Yet the triple hare motif, three circular hares linked by their ears, representing death, redemption and rebirth, is sometimes seen in churches. Given its trickster appellation, it seems fitting that the hare has a paradoxical aspect to its nature.

There is mystery also in the sarsen stones that can be found in Bracketts Coppice and the surrounding fields. These stones are sometimes solitary, sometimes in groups. There are places in the corners of fields or woods where they have been cleared from the farmland and piled together. Sarsen stones, oolitic limestone, granite and stones of other geological formulation seem to have been revered by our distant predecessors. Maybe they were seen as holding a deep and subtle kind of consciousness or possibly, when in circles or rows, they represented the spirits. Whether dressed and erected as standing stones or stone circles or whether found randomly strewn as glacial deposits as here, they suggest a link with ancient times, of ancestors and hidden gods. One of the joys of Bracketts Coppice is finding these stones, half-hidden in gnarled woods and nestling in the soft gloaming of meadowland

EAST CHELBOROUGH AND LEWCOMBE
A Fairy Hill and Wayward Church

OS maps: Explorer 117 or Landranger 194

Grid refs: Castle Hill ST552054, Church ST559076

Directions: From Evershot go west on the Beaminster road for approx. 1½ miles and take the second right to Chelborough. After approx. 1 mile Castle Hill is clearly visible on your left. The hill is on private farmland so must be viewed from the road. For St James' Church, Lewcombe, continue along the road for approx. 1½ miles and just after Oakland's Farm turn right opposite the Oakborough Herd sign, down the long drive to Lewcombe Manor. After the second cattle-grid, fork left to the church. The nearby manor house and grounds are private, but limited parking is possible near the church.

Nearby refreshments: Village store, Halstock; Talbot Arms, Benville; Acorn Inn, Evershot

East Chelborough is a hamlet consisting of two farms and a couple of fine period houses. In the yard of Stake Farm are the ruins of a motte and bailey and behind the farmhouse is Castle Hill, marked on OS maps as another motte and bailey, where once there was a mediaeval castle, possibly built on prehistoric foundations. This hill has a curious legend attached to it, for it is a fairy hill and the fairies are jealous of any intrusion.

Centuries ago, when East Chelborough was larger than it is today, legend has it that the villagers planned to build a small church at the foot of Castle Hill. However, every morning the stones were found to have been moved a few miles away to Lewcombe. This place was by the banks of a stream that had halted any further progress, earth fairies being unable to cross running water. Perhaps the fairies objected to a church being built at Castle Hill because the building would have blocked a fairy path, or maybe the hill was inhabited by the 'good folk' and it was felt that Christianity was at odds with the otherworldly domain.

Painting 6: A glimpse of St James Church, Lewcombe. The little church, surrounded by trees and ancient graves, retains an air of peaceful seclusion, broken only by the murmur of the stream that flows nearby.

Eventually the villagers became tired of the futility of their task and the church was built in Lewcombe.

The world of the fairies has both repelled and fascinated people for generations. Fairies are the strange beings of folklore, sometimes quasi-human in appearance and credited with having magical powers. There are various definitions as to what fairies are. In Victorian times there was a strand of thought that saw fairies as an ancestral conquered race living in hiding in an in-between world. They had light, changeable bodies yet were able to manifest physically. Or perhaps they are part of the spiritual realm of the land, the legendary shape-changing people of enchantment, acting as guardian spirits. Over time, the definitions of and names for fairies have changed according to culture and physical location. The one thing that seems to be universally agreed is that fairies are tricky entities, with a penchant for deluding mankind. Placatory gestures were often offered, and in rustic England, bowls of milk were nightly placed for the nourishment of the Brownie, an action that would ensure easy housekeeping and a placid home.

Fairies of bleak moorland are different from those of woodland and meadow. The wilder hills and mountains host one type of fairy, such as the Highland *Am Fear Glas Mor* (Big Grey Man of Mac Dhui), which witnesses have attested to standing over 3 m tall, while fairies of the glades and meadows have been seen as slight slim beings. Some fairy sightings, such as the Owl Man of Mawnan Smith in Cornwall, are so weird that they almost decry description. This creature, seen near the church by a couple of schoolgirls in 1977 and latterly by other people, is described as having an owl-like head with two glaring eyes and black pincer-like feet. The church could possibly have been built on an earlier pagan site, which might be a reason for these strange sightings in this area.

The Sidhe, the Tuatha de Danaan, the Gentry – these are some of the names the Irish give to the 'good folk'. Fairy lore in Ireland, although now diminishing, if not utterly diminished, has held out longer than it has in Britain. The hawthorn or May tree is known as the fairy tree and in Ireland country people respect the lone, aged hawthorn growing in a rough field, for fairy trees are sacrosanct to the 'little people' and harm may come to those who disturb or damage leaf, branch or trunk. At the end of the 19th century, Lady Augusta Gregory collated the rich fairy lore of Ireland, ensuring that this particular tradition would not be lost. Katharine Briggs working in the mid-20th century compiled a similar body of work on fairies in the British Isles.

All countries have their fairies, giving them different names and descriptions but essentially recognising the same qualities. These beings are both corporeal and incorporeal; they perform the function of tricky mediators between the world of spirit and the physical world (they themselves dwelling in an intermediate realm between the two). They are similar but a different class of being from the nature spirits, such as the Faunus from Roman lore. Nature spirits are exemplified in their maximum sense by the Greek god Pan. These types of spirits lack the flexibility of fairies and are more tied to significant features in the landscape, such as a grove of trees, spring or pile of rocks. Modern Western culture has eradicated any fairy belief, but other cultures still recognise this particular type and class of being, seeing them as no less natural as humanity.

At the end of the long drive adjacent to Lewcombe Manor is the reputedly fairy-chosen site of the church of St James. It has partly 16th and partly 18th century features, with a large circular Victorian stained glass window depicting angelic hosts being a notable addition. The font is 18th century and unusually situated in front of the communion rails. The church is small but encapsulates a subtle modest beauty. The name of where it is situated, 'Lewcombe', is evocative of the Welsh god Lew or Lleu, 'the Shining One'. This god of sun and light has similarities, in some ways at least, with Jesus, for Lleu starts to come into life at the winter solstice, a few days before Christmas. It could be that the position of the church is one of synthesis.

EGGARDON HILL
The Bell Stone and Strange Occurrences

OS maps: Explorer 117 or Landranger 194

Grid refs: Eggardon Hill crossroads/parking SY547947, Bell Stone SY536951

Directions: Take the A35 east from Bridport and after approx. 2½ miles, at Vinney Cross, turn left to Spyway and Maiden Newton. Approx. 1½ miles after the Spyway Inn, Eggardon Hill is evident on your left. There are numerous parking options along the road and at the crossroads atop the hill. The Neolithic henge and tumuli are immediately northwest of the crossroads. From the crossroads walk approx. 100 m down the Powerstock road, then take the footpath southwest across the field to the Eggardon Hill 'entrance', but do NOT enter. Instead continue walking around and down the southern flanks of the hill. The Bell Stone sits below the second major outcrop of rock in the hillside to your right.

Nearby refreshments: Spyway Inn, Askerswell; Three Horseshoes, Powerstock; Marquis of Lorne, Nettlecombe

Eggardon Hill is a prominent chalk escarpment crowned with the remains of a large Iron Age fort. Although not of the size of Maiden Castle near Dorchester, it is an impressive structure nonetheless. The view from the heights is sublime and the wildwood of Powerstock Common covers the near distance. A few Bronze Age tumuli are still visible on the hilltop and the whole area carries a sense of haunted history. Through the middle of the fort led the pathway to the gallows, first erected in the Middle Ages, at a height where they could be seen from afar, the grim sight serving as a ghastly warning that life could be cut short by crimes as seemingly petty as sheep stealing.

Before Eggardon was transformed into a fort there was earlier activity of a strange and intriguing nature. By the crossroads is an unusual Neolithic feature – a henge in the form of a circular raised bank. Henges denote a sacred area, a temple, a place devoted to worship and/or regarded as a dwelling place of a god or gods. There is a barrow in the middle of the henge and the construction is similar to a ring barrow, except that the henge is larger than usual, as if the barrow were not the main focal point. It is thought that ring barrows mainly contained female inhumations. Hundreds of years later in the Bronze Age, a barrow was actually built into the henge, maybe as a mark of respect. It lines up with at least two other barrows that lie on the edge of the field. This area was a place of ritual and continuation for a long time. The highest part of Eggardon lies further on and for that reason this site is partly sheltered. Maybe that is why early people built their temple and memorials to the dead here. Or perhaps this piece of land was charged with a certain type of subtle earth energy.

At the crossroads, the rough lane leading west is a continuation of the

Roman road coming from the east. Strange occurrences have happened here, particularly in the evening and at night. In 1974 a blue hovering light was seen by a man driving along this lane. His car stalled, but when the blue light eventually disappeared, his car started again. Horses and dogs have been spooked by something unseen but obviously felt. Cars and watches stop and then start after a short time, and men's voices have been faintly heard, shouting, as if in battle. On the actual hilltop there is also supernatural activity, for there are tales of Diana's Wild Hunt racing by, hounds baying for the souls of the dead. Lights have been seen hanging over the hill and there have been various reports of a white stag, UFOs and fairies.

On the southern lower flanks of Eggardon are some white rocky outcrops with large boulders strewn beneath them. One of these boulders, standing alone, is known as the Bell Stone, but its old name was probably Bel Stone, from the Celtic god Belinos, a solar deity, equivalent in many ways to the Greek god Apollo. Known as 'the Bright One', his rites recognised the power of the god to fertilise the land at springtime. Seen also as a pastoral deity, part of the rites dedicated to his name included the driving of cattle through the fire in order to protect them from disease. In a seeming reversal of attribution, some sources also recognise Belinos as a god of the Underworld and of the dead.

On May Eve, also known as Beltane, the pagan bale-fire was lit on Bellstone Ledge, an outcrop above this stone. Flickering in the half-light, the flames were a living force and testament to the power of heat and light. They shone as a salutation to the power of the sun and the life force that the sun engendered. It is attested that a few villages in various parts of the country still burn this

fire and people jump over the flames as an act of purification. Tradition has it that nine different woods went into the making of the bale-fire – oak, birch, fir, willow, rowan, apple, grapevine, hazel and hawthorn. These trees represent, in the above order, god, goddess, birth, death, magic, love, joy, wisdom and purity, respectively.

Eggardon Hill is a place of energy and splendour. Magnificent at any time of the year, its presence influences the landscape for many miles around. Its large totem bulk is a distinctive feature and if any place can be considered as a place of power, this is one.

LEIGH
An Intriguing Village

OS maps: Explorer 117 or Landranger 194

Grid refs: Cross ST621086, Church ST618087, Miz-maze ST620082, Pound ST616083

Directions: Leigh is well-signed to the east of the A37 approx. 12 miles north of Dorchester. Drive to the eastern end of the village to see the stone cross at the three-way junction. Back-track just past the church, turn left into South Street and park near the far end of the lane. To view the miz-maze, walk up the drive towards White Hall Farm, then use the footpath to skirt around the south side of the house and farm. The outline of the maze is visible atop the second field. The Pound is almost directly opposite the southern end of South Street.

Nearby refreshments: Garage stores, Leigh; Wriggles Farm Produce Shop and Chetnole Inn, Chetnole; Rest and Welcome Inn, Melbury Osmund

The miz-maze at Leigh (pronounced 'Lie') is a rare feature, as there are only eight such turf mazes still surviving in England, and only three are so named, the other two being at Breamore and Winchester in Hampshire. All that remains in Leigh is a low bank in the highest part of the field with a faint mound in the middle (the bank used to be much higher but now is slight, standing at 2 ft). The maze is depicted on four old maps: an Elizabethan map dated 1569–74, a map dating from 1620, the Isaac Taylor Map of Dorset 1705 and Bayly's Map of Dorset 1773. The depictions all vary slightly, but the maze is definitely marked as a feature in the landscape. An aerial photograph taken in 1986 shows the outer bank to be hexagonal but no traces of the turf paths can be seen. There is a preservation order on the site, so restoration is a possibility.

The Leigh maze is considered to be one of the 'lost' mazes of Dorset. Others (now gone) were at Bere Regis, 'Troy Town' near Dorchester, and another near Pimperne, which was described by the antiquary John Aubrey as having a unique design. Sadly it was ploughed up in 1730. 'Troy Town' is a name for mazes derived from the idea that the walls of the city of Troy were constructed

Miz-maze near Breamore House, Fordingbridge, Hants.

in such a complex way that any enemy would be unable to find their way out. Many turf mazes are sited near a holy well and, interestingly, there is said to be a well in a nearby cottage garden (private), a well that has 13 steps down to it, an unusual feature. Leigh is on one of the old pilgrim routes to Glastonbury and the well could have provided refreshment for pilgrims on their journey.

The complicated paths of the miz-maze at Leigh could be seen until the 19th century. Before 1800 it stood on unenclosed common land, but in 1800 the land was enclosed and the new owner had little interest in the maze and through lack of upkeep it began its slow deterioration. The jolly May festivities that were held around the maze died away and the young men who, up until this time, accompanied by feasting and drinking, used to scour the trenches of the maze every few years so that it could be walked or even danced upon, found other activities to let off steam.

The earliest known maze in Ireland and the British Isles is found incised in AD 550 on a boulder in County Wicklow. This is known as the Hollywood Stone, the name possibly a derivation of 'Holy Wood'. In Rocky Valley near Tintagel are two small depictions of labyrinths on a rock face, the dating of which is uncertain – they could possibly be Bronze Age. The difference between a maze and a labyrinth is that a maze has a choice of paths and a labyrinth has only one. Turf mazes are also difficult to date as although the patterns might be ancient, mazes need to be regularly re-cut, an activity that disturbs any archaeological evidence. Many of the mazes in northern Europe are marked by stones rather than cut turf paths. Some of these stone mazes were constructed to entrap evil spirits, rather like the web-like 'spirit catchers' of the Native Americans.

From 'A Midsummer Night's Dream' by William Shakespeare:

The nine men's Morris is fill'd up with mud
And the quaint images in the wanton green
For lack of tread are undistinguishable.

'Treading the maze' was an activity that probably originally had initiatory overtones, marking a map of creation. It is possible that the seven rings of paths were linked with the planets. The outer path represented Earth and the final inner circular ring the Sun. They probably mark the site of prehistoric dancing grounds. British mazes have parallels with Egyptian and Cretan labyrinths, both in design and meaning. The rituals of life, death and fertility have been linked to the festivals in which the maze forms the central part. Within Celtic paganism the symbol of the maze has been found carved on rocks and the bosses of shields. The maze is such a powerful symbol that it was adopted by Christianity, with a fine example being seen in Chartres Cathedral near Paris. Within the Christian ethos, the maze was seen as the meanderings of the soul's journey towards the 'Heavenly City' or the completion of life's journey, culminating in union with God.

On the 1620 map, the common land where the maze is situated in Leigh is named 'Witches Corner'. For hundreds of years witches were said to gather and hold their rites here, observing the old Sabbaths. It is said that the last witch in England was arrested at this spot, tried in Dorchester and burnt at Maumbury Rings, an ancient henge monument dating from Neolithic times, which was the place of numerous executions. Interestingly, a modern close on the east side of Leigh is called Miz Maze.

Leigh has another interesting artefact – the remains of a mainly mediaeval cross at the main junction in the village. This cross probably originally came from the church and is thought to have been erected here around the mid-19th century. This type of cross, of which there are further examples at Rampisham and Bradford Abbas, sometimes served the community as a place where the Gospel was preached to the general populace. There are also the remains of another old cross in the churchyard, south east of the church underneath the yew tree.

The church at Leigh, dedicated to St Andrew, has some interesting carvings on the tower. One of them, seemingly a cleric with his hands in prayer, I thought at first was a Sheela-na-Gig. Sheela-na-Gigs are grotesque female figures squatting with their legs apart and have an ancient heritage, but their roots are hard to verify. Found on European, Irish and British churches from the 11th century onwards, there are different opinions as to their meaning. The

Celtic scholar Dr Anne Ross ascribes them to the mother goddess and a fertility religion. Others suggest they are a warning against the corrupting influence of lust. Or as a figure of a hag they represent the Cailleach, an Irish goddess. It is said the Devil flees at the sight of a vulva, so perhaps the figures, particularly if sited above a door or window, serve as a protective device, warding off evil.

The Pound is almost directly opposite the southern end of South Street. The brass plaque there explains its purpose:

> *The Pound*
> *(Dating from around AD 1695)*
>
> *This Pound was provided by manorial custom for the impounding of livestock which strayed from the commons and closes, causing damage in the open arable fields. Once impounded, animals could only be repossessed on payment of a fine*

Leigh is a small and seemingly insignificant village, but it contains a plethora of bizarre and interesting things. It serves as an example and reminder that behind a seemingly modest façade, many villages deserve more than a cursory glance.

LITTLEBREDY
Bridehead Lake

OS maps: Explorer OL15 or Landranger 194

Grid refs: Parking SY587891, Lake SY588888

Directions: Just west of Winterbourne Abbas on the A35 turn for Littlebredy. On reaching the village, pass the church on your left and park near the unusual shelter. Walk 50 m down the hill and take Church Walk on the left running in front of some cottages. Bear right at the church to the lake and waterfall. Only part of the lake grounds are open to the public, so do not wander onto the private sections and leave the grounds as immaculately as you find them. Please heed the signs by making a donation towards the upkeep of the church.

Nearby refreshments: Abbotsbury, Portesham and Winterbourne Abbas

Littlebredy, pronounced 'Briddy' in the local dialect, is beautifully positioned in the Bride valley. Surrounded by hills, the village has remained mainly free of modern housing and has kept its integrity as an estate village, clustered around the church and manor house. In the *Domesday Book* it was written that the wealthy Abbey of Cerne Abbas held Littlebredy Manor. After the dissolution of the monasteries the Abbey sold the land, and in 1544 Philip Vanwilder acquired the Littlebredy estate. Various owners held the manor during the next couple of centuries until in the late 18th century Robert Williams, a banker who worked in London and who already owned extensive areas of land, bought it. The Williams family had connections with Dorset as generations of Williams had lived in Winterborne Herringston.

The family still lives in the manor house, Bridehead. They effected a few changes, extending the house and replacing the old mediaeval cottages with ones providing greater comfort. The grounds surrounding the house were landscaped and the springs dammed to provide a lake. The lake is a focal point for the community, as large bodies of water tend to be. The old marshy area of the

springs has been transformed into the clearest of waters. Fed by the unceasing flow, the lake empties as a waterfall that forms the beginnings of the lovely River Bride. The water also supplies the local manor and the village.

Twenty years or so ago a local tenant farmer introduced trout to the lake. These trout still glide in the lake, huge and quite tame. In the clear waters they can be easily spotted. Fish, especially trout and salmon, have a special association with holy wells. They are seen as guardians holding the knowledge of the gods and seeds of wisdom, the place of Formation where springs originate – that strange place of beginnings, of spirits and the roots of things. This lake has the ability to be seen as an enormous well, powered by waters that were probably once considered holy. A river starts the beginning of its journey as a spring, coming out of the earth or rocks as a small flow of water. The place where the waters are rising is special, like a natural font. The early Celtic Christian church used springs and wells as places of baptism and it was only when the power of the church moved to Rome that the font became fixed inside the church building.

A quality to be found here is the feeling of tranquillity that is one of the special gifts that lakes bestow. The Celts saw lakes as a gateway to the world of the gods, an entrance to another sort of reality. Strange beings were attributed to lakes; there were monsters such as the Scottish Kelpie or Water Horse who would snatch the unwary into the dark depths, there to be eaten. The Loch Ness Monster is another example of a lake oddity and many Scottish lochs have their equivalents, strange beings that have been glimpsed but never defined. The Irish poet and scholar W.B. Yeats thought that creatures were placed in lakes to guard 'the gates of wisdom'.

Bronze Age and later Celtic Iron Age people deposited placatory offerings in lakes. As lakes were seen as portals, these offerings were to the gods and ancestors, particularly in times of strife, to try to effect supernatural aid. One of the best-known sites, where many offerings have been found, is Flag Fen near Peterborough. Walkways were made over the water by driving oak timbers into the muddy depths, and from these raised wooden track-ways were thrown valuable bronze and iron goods, including swords, daggers, spears, shields, cauldrons and jewellery. Druids on Ynys Mon, otherwise known as Anglesey, made huge deposits of valuable items in Llyn Cerrig Bach over a 250-year period up to the 1st century AD. The quality and craftsmanship of the more than 150 items recovered from the lake have exceeded anything yet found.

The archetypal image of the Lady of the Lake, receiving in her pellucid hand Arthur's famed sword Excalibur, is linked with the idea of lakes as receptacles and revealers of the Otherworld. The Lake District epitomises the inspirational quality that lakes have. There is something in the human psyche that responds to large, deep, still bodies of water, particularly if these waters reflect surrounding hills and mountains. The reflected world is a different world, a captured one, a doppelganger. Although the lake here is largely excavated, it works so beautifully within its landscape that it seems perfectly natural and right.

The name 'Bride' for the river could come from the Celtic *bridda* meaning gushing. Bride is also the name of a widely worshipped Celtic goddess in pre-Christian Britain. Known as 'the Exalted One', Bride tended the triple fires of smith craft, and was associated with healing and poetry. She was also connected to sacred springs and wells. Her festival, Imbolc, falls on 2 February and celebrates the early beginnings of spring.

LITTON CHENEY
An Early Downland Settlement

OS maps: Explorer OL15 or Landranger 194

Grid refs: Pins Knoll ST541905, Church ST552907

Directions: On the A35 heading west, ignore the sign to Litton Cheney, then approx. 2 miles further on ignore the crossroads signed to West Compton. Take the next left (unsigned) and drop down the steep narrow lane. Pause at the sharp left bend to view Pins Knoll on your right. Continue on down the lane and park at the main junction in the village, near the bus shelter.

Nearby refreshments: White Horse Inn, Litton Cheney

Litton Cheney is a typical Bride valley village. People have found this area a pleasant place from prehistoric times and various early settlement sites have been discovered. North of the village is an embanked enclosure thought at

first to be a ritual henge monument, but excavations in the 1970s concluded it was a late Neolithic farmstead, later used as a Bronze Age cemetery. Farming reached Britain in early Neolithic times (around 4800 BC). Simple crops such as emmer, a type of grain, oats and barley were grown and sheep, goats and cattle kept. People lived in wooden rectangular huts that later were replaced by circular structures, such as the excavated remains of the farmstead found here. The village of Litton Cheney has been designated a conservation area, so

that the ratio of old to new buildings favours the old. A stream runs in front of many of the cottages and this stream and others nearby give freshness and vitality to the area, the cheerful gurgling of the waters adding a lilting charm.

The parish church, dedicated to St Mary, is a fine Grade I Listed building situated in a commanding position overlooking the village. The oldest parts of the building date from the early 14th century and comprise sections of the nave including the south doorway and porch. The tower was built later in the same century. Inside the tower there is an interesting clock *circa* 1700 that has no hand or dials and just uses a striker to sound the hour. The church was restored in 1878 but still retains its character despite the Victorian facelift. Inside, near the south door, is an unusual brass memorial plaque. Dated 1681 it is inscribed:

Here lyeth the body of Anna Henbill who exchanged this life for a better in the 25th yeare of her age. Beneath this stone in a dark dusty bed (lamented much) a virgin rests her head. An such an one who (dying) hath bereft the world of that worth as scarce in it is left. Of a sweet face but of a sweeter minde, and a sweet frame (dying) shee left behinde, smitten by death even in her blooming age, and the height of beauty. She went off y stage of this frail world with grief. We see that such rare creatures seldome aged be, for why the angels want such company to join with them in heavenly melody, with whom in heaven she does now possess the fruit of virtue's lasting happiness.

Nothing much is known about this presumably lovely and much loved young woman. The poignant inscription suggests she was yet to experience the full round of life; that she was unmarried and struck down in her prime by disease or accident. At least she had the delight of living, if only for a while, in this bucolic and wistful area.

Just half a mile west of Litton Cheney, near the sharp corner up Chalk

Pit Lane, is the distinctive Pins Knoll. Parking is difficult, but the hill can be clearly seen from the road. The Knoll is private ground, but a public footpath is immediately adjacent to it and provides exceptional views towards Bridport. It is a flat-topped hill jutting out over the valley and an Iron Age site dating from around 700 BC, which over hundreds of years became, with the influx of the Romans, Romano-British.

There has been a certain amount of excavation at this site, with various finds including a burial of the 1st century AD, one of several burials that were probably of the local Durotriges tribe. Grave goods found included part of a sheep as well as the customary clay food vessel so that the departed might have sustenance in the land of the dead.

LONG BREDY
Martin's Down and Our Hidden Ancestors

OS maps: Explorer OL15 or Landranger 194

Grid refs: Parking ST571906, Bank barrow ST572912

Directions: Approx. 3 miles west of Winterbourne Abbas on the A35, turn south to Long Bredy. Turn left at the bottom of the hill and at the end of the walled section of road, as it bends sharply right, turn left (signed 'Church only') and park near the church. Take the footpath to the left of the church up Long Barrow Hill to the trig point and the bank barrow. There are numerous other barrows, tumuli and ancient features across Martin's Down, and Black Down to the southeast. Turning right at the end of the barrow will create a circular walk back down to the right-hand side of the church. One of the best but often missed views of the barrow is by car when driving along the A35.

Nearby refreshments: Askerswell, Litton Cheney and Winterbourne Abbas

Martin's Down runs adjacent to an ancient ridgeway track (now the A35). It is a ceremonial and burial site that was in use for thousands of years. Dominating the area is the almost 200-m (645-ft)-long 'bank' barrow, which is clearly visible when driving along the A35. It is much longer than a more conventional 'long' barrow such as the one to the southeast. It may also be the second longest in the country and it is certainly one of the most clearly defined.

Long barrows such as this were built in Neolithic times around 4000–2500 BC. Bank barrows differ from long barrows in that they do not seem to have an internal burial chamber. Only very few bank barrows are thought to exist in England, and Dorset seems to have more than its fair share, with the eroded remains of two more in this area above Littlebredy and others at Maiden Castle, Broadmayne and possibly Pentridge. Archaeological studies at other bank barrow sites suggest it is possible they used for the excarnation of the dead prior to the bones being interred in a barrow. Sometimes burials have been found in the ditches that are invariably found alongside barrow earthworks. When viewed from the southeast the bank barrow near Long Bredy forms a false horizon, behind which, at midsummer, the sun sinks out of sight. Thus movements of the sun may have been a consideration when building this structure.

There is another Martin's Down by the Dorset/Hampshire border near the tiny village of Pentridge, which holds a rare and fascinating earthwork known as the Dorset Cursus, dating from 3300 BC. It consists of two distinct earthen banks forming either a straightish line or an elliptical circle with a terminus either side. They are so named because William Stukely, an 18th-century antiquarian, on seeing the cursus near Stonehenge thought it might be a racecourse. The Dorset Cursus is the longest in the country, extending about 10 km (6 miles). The earlier southern bank is known as the Gussage Cursus and the northern bank as the Pentridge Cursus. The earthwork runs between Thickthorn Down on Cranborne Chase and the East Dorset Martin's Down. At each end there would have been the terminal bank, now disappeared, joining the two sides of the cursus.

The Great Cursus near Stonehenge is the better known and more intensively excavated. There has been dispute over the usage of cursuses, with one thought that they could be spirit paths or an 'avenue for the dead' as they seem to be a link between barrows, particularly long barrows. These enigmatic structures are often built at transitional places, such as areas of fusion of different geology or at the confluence of two rivers. Maybe they provided a place where shamans would practise 'spirit flight' or they were the stage for an initiatory ordeal of some sort.

Most of the archaeological sites on Martin's Down and the immediate area consist of individual Bronze Age barrows. There are also two standing stones on the other side of the A35 and a stone circle, the Nine Stones, and another long barrow west of Winterbourne Abbas. The number of barrows and earthworks in this area is significant and is similar to the density of barrows around Stonehenge. These features are emblematic of a focused vision and a vividly held belief system. At Martin's Down, Stonehenge and Avebury are huge votive religious sites moulding the landscape. The thousands of hours spent creating these structures of stone and earth and the commitment and vision manifested in these ceremonial places we cannot challenge or rebuke. Something helpfully instructive is revealed – that enthusiasm fuelled by spiritual conviction can produce superhuman results. Much has gone from Martin's Down, eradicated by erosion or the plough, yet there is still a power

in this place, still a memory of different gods, different ways of thinking and living, different needs for survival. Yet somewhere deep in our DNA lies their DNA. These people are our ancestors and their thoughts lie buried in our memories.

LOSCOMBE AND BURCOMBE
A Lost Combe and 'Cunning Man'

OS maps: Explorer 117 or Landranger 194

Grid refs: Loscombe DWT car park SY502979, Burcombe SY518988

Directions: Approx. 3 miles north of Bridport on the A3066 turn right at the Half Moon Inn, then after ½ a mile right again to Loscombe. At the bottom of the steep narrow lane and after two 90-degree corners (left then right) take the left fork. Approx. 250 m on the right enter and park in the small grass DWT Nature Reserve car park. It is possible to walk to and from Burcombe via a number of different circular routes, of varying terrain of approx. 4–6 km. To get to Burcombe by car drive back to the T-junction, turn left up the long narrow lane, then turn again along the aptly named Ridgeback Lane to South Poorton. Continue on to North Poorton, then down the narrow lane to Burcombe. Parking is limited.

Nearby refreshments: Half Moon Inn, Melplash; Sawmill Café, Mapperton House

Loscombe and Burcombe are two hamlets encompassed by a variety of small hills that were probably inspirational to the strange and enigmatic figure John Walsh. Living in the mid-16th century, Walsh was known as the 'Cunning Man' of Netherbury. Cunning is derived from the Anglo-Saxon *cunus*, which means 'to know'. 'Cunning' people were considered as having the gift for 'going over', being able to enter an altered reality. The cunning man and the female equivalent, the wise woman, used their gifts to help their community, working as seers, healers and advisors. Walsh would also have been the recipient of a handed-down belief system, which recognised the value of plant remedies. Woods and open country were seen as being full of healing herbs, to be made into salves and potions. The landscape also contained fairies and nature spirits, along with

other beings and entities, both benign and malevolent. For those with the 'sight' these beings could be seen – not with the physical eye but with the inner eye, the same vehicle that allows dreams to be recognised in a quasi-visual sense.

There were times when such communicators with the unseen world were held in respect by the local community and times when there was suspicion and fear. The text in the *Bible* 'Thou shalt not suffer a witch to live' was an ever-present threat, influencing both opinion and the law. In 1566 Walsh was sent to trial, where under interrogation he claimed to have communicated with the fairies, an activity that was seen as witchcraft.

> *He being demanded how he knoweth when anye man is bewitched: He sayeth*
> *that he knew it partlye by the Feries, white, green and black. Which when he is*
> *disposed to use, hee speaketh with them upon hyls, where as there is great heapes*
> *of earth, as namely in Dorsetshire. And between the houres of 12 and one at noone*
> *or at midnight he useth them. Whereof he sayeth the blacke Feries be the worst.*

From the trial of John Walsh

Noon and midnight are liminal times at the end of one cycle and beginning of another. These in-between times and in-between places, like crossroads, the sea shore and hilltops, are thought to be portals to the 'Other'. If any hills could be said to be 'fairy hills' they must be the evocative hills around here. The route Walsh took was probably the old Coffin Way, also known as Dead Man's Lane, which led from Netherbury up over the hills in the direction of Mapperton and on towards Loscombe and Burcombe.

Loscombe, the 'lost combe', lies deep in the shady tranquillity of a steep vale. It has no church, just a few cottages and a couple of farms. The Dorset Wildlife Trust tends a portion of land here, which comprises mostly ancient hedgerows surrounding unimproved grassland, part of which slopes down to a stream and an accompanying area of wetland. Snake-Head Fritillaries, those strange and most intriguing of spring flowers, grow here, and in two fields at the eastern end of the reserve the land is bumpy with the anthills of yellow

meadow ants. Loscombe and Burcombe are situated in a relatively untouched landscape. Burcombe, stuck on the end of a tiny lane that ambles down the valley from North Poorton, is hardly big enough to be even described as a hamlet, containing as it does just a farm and few cottages. Most of the fields are pasture because the steep hills and deep valleys make ploughing almost impossible.

This part of West Dorset is a landscape within a larger landscape, a self-contained parcel of land that has all the ingredients of a latter-day Arcadia. If the haunting pipes of Pan could be heard anywhere in this county it would be here, trilling from a hillside wood in the blue dusk of a late summer evening. Country folk talk of 'whistling up' the fairies. I have tried this and my whistle was immediately answered by the mimicking call of a bird, or something that sounded like a bird! The Irish tin whistle is thought of as a fairy instrument and there is an Irish aire that is said to come from the fairies. Ireland is still a country where in remote areas, in the gloaming of the approaching night, whistle music can be heard, shrilly rising from a fastness where no human has set foot. A friend of mine, the late Martin Doyle, heard such music strangely issuing forth from a deep dell in the wilds of County Cork. The unearthly quality was such that he knew no human agency was involved and fear came upon him and he ran, until the notes became faint and the music was gone.

There is a barrow on one of the hills that overlooks Burcombe and another on Knight's Hill to the south of Loscombe. These qualify as the 'great heapes of earth' that John Walsh said were the abode of the fairies, and the setting of both these hilltop barrows would be suitable as an aid for invocation, for hills and woods surround them and at the time of Walsh no buildings were near. Under a full moon, careening into and out of the wilderness, careening in and out of the sensibility of the cunning man, the fairy hordes would manifest their wyrd wisdom and Walsh would look and listen, translating the strangeness into the language of human understanding.

LYME REGIS
Monmouth Beach

OS maps: Explorer 116 or Landranger 193

Grid ref: Parking SY337916

Directions: Use one of the car parks near the Cobb. Monmouth Beach lies to the west of here below the Undercliff, partly fronted by the dinghy park and beach huts. The beach becomes more rugged as you walk west.

Monmouth Beach is named in memory of the young but doomed Duke of Monmouth, illegitimate son of Charles II. He landed here, from exile in The Netherlands, with just three boats and 82 men on 11 June 1685, claiming the throne for the Protestant cause from his Catholic uncle James II. Although Monmouth gained some support, he was defeated at the Battle of Sedgemoor in Somerset on 6 July and beheaded in London on the 15th. Twelve Lyme men who had supported him were hung, drawn and quartered on Monmouth Beach. This barbaric form of execution served as a warning to others who might be tempted to veer from the established order.

The Undercliff, the broken land above the beach, provides a wild backdrop to the shore. Landslips have formed this unique terrain, with historically the largest being the slip on Christmas Eve in 1830, the Bindon landslip. Torrential rain formed a mudslide, which caused a huge slab of land to drop towards the sea, creating a deep chasm. The fallen land became known as Goat Island,

after the sheep and goats that used to graze there. The wooded unstable cliffs meander towards the west, trees and bushes growing haphazardly down to the edge of the pebbly sand. Sometimes the shifting land causes a tree's purchase to fail and invariably they fall, flayed branches and sturdy trunks eventually becoming bleached hulks, ossifying in the sun and salt sea spray. Winter storms push driftwood up high on the beach, to be collected as fuel by locals or used by artists and craftspeople, who appreciate the qualities that prolonged immersion in salt water brings to wood.

Blue lias rock shelves studded with ammonites form a causeway stretching far into the waves. Pools are revealed at low tide, holding a few small crabs, tiny sullen elusive fish and shyly inquisitive prawns. 'Inquisitive' could also be applied to the fossil hunters who often come to this beach. Bent over, they chip-chip away at a promising rock, hoping to find the half-hidden testament of an ancient life form turned to stone. Many fossils are found just lying on the beach. The seashore is a liminal place, where two different elements meet, water and earth. A favourite subject of artists and poets, the shore suggests a fusion within the landscape of two major life forms, the sea and the land. To mystics, this meeting, whether placid or of titanic storm, is seen as a visionary matrix.

This is easily the quietest of Lyme's beaches, beautiful in all seasons and dog-friendly. It is best visited at low tide when the flat rocks are revealed, offering themselves up as broad pavements for walking. Stroll a half-mile or so west and any human clamour dies away, to be replaced by the rhythmic sound of waves and the rough screeching of gulls.

LYME REGIS
St Michael's Church and Leper's Well

OS maps: Explorer 117 or Landranger 193

Grid refs: Church SY343922, Well SY341922

Directions: St Michael's Church is 100 m north of the Tourist Information Centre. There is parking nearby, but it is a pleasant walk from the previous entry 'Monmouth Beach' along the Esplanade to the church. For the well, take Monmouth Street opposite the church. Fork right at the memorial garden and directly in front of you take Riverside Walk to the Town Mill. Follow the footpath to the right of the Mill for 50 m, cross a small bridge and the well is on your right.

Lyme Regis is an ancient town and being south-facing and comfortably situated in a sheltered valley was probably inhabited in prehistoric times. Certainly the Romans came here, naming the town *Lym Supra Mare* (*Lym* after the river that flows through the town and *Supra Mare* meaning 'above sea/water'. The earliest recorded mention of Lyme was in AD 774 when King Cynewulf of the West Saxons granted the town and some land along the River Lym to Sherborne Abbey. Monks from the Abbey initiated a sea-salt manufacturing industry. Once the Cobb was built in the 13th century, protecting the small harbour from storms, more industries flourished. Lyme became a busy port and, with fishing and boat building also playing an important role, the small town's fortunes began to rise.

Edward I bequeathed a Royal Charter on the town in 1284 and Lyme became Lyme Regis. By the 18th century it had become a popular and fashionable seaside resort, frequented by Royalty, smart society, artists and writers. Jane Austen

spent time here, as did the painters Turner and Whistler. Mary Anning, a local girl with an interest in fossils, found the complete fossil of an Ichthyosaurus (the 'fish-lizard'). This fostered further interest in the town.

The church of St Michael is arrestingly sited on a small bluff overlooking the sea. The land has eroded over the centuries and the church is now much nearer the sea than in Saxon times. Churches dedicated to St Michael are often found on high places and craggy peaks. St Michael is one of the Archangels of the Four Quarters, his domain being the south, and he is known as the leader of God's host. Similar to St George, he defeated the dragon. The dragon in early Christian times represented the earlier pagan religions, which were seen as evil. As Christ was recognised as all-conquering, chapels and churches were often built on pagan sites, destroying what had gone before. Michael (meaning 'like unto God') is described as a chief or great prince, and he is well known for casting out the Devil. It is also possible that the church was erected on the site of an early temple dedicated to Michael in his solar aspect or sacred to a god or goddess of the sea. Michael's roots are pre-Christian and his chief correspondence is with the Elemental Fire, giving him the attributes of a Sun god.

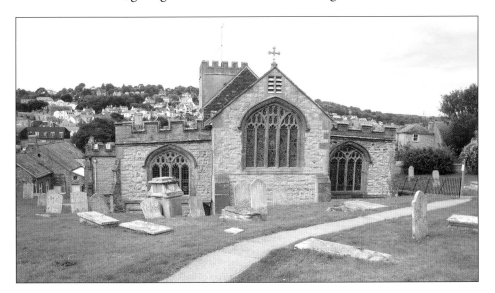

For those familiar with the concept of ley lines, said to be lines of energy that criss-cross the land, it is proposed that there is a very powerful line that crosses England from east to west, ending at St Michael's Mount in Cornwall. This line of force is called the Michael Line and it travels through many sites dedicated to St Michael (though the church at Lyme Regis is not one of these), such as churches developed from hilltop shrines, examples being Glastonbury Tor and Brentor on Dartmoor. Some of the major prehistoric sites in Britain, often with an unknown dedication, such as Stonehenge, are also said to be conduits for the Michael Force.

Christianity was first introduced to Britain during the Roman occupation. This Romano-British Christianity was in competition with the vestiges of the native paganism and the introduced northern religions of the Norse people and Saxons. During the Dark Ages, after the Romans left these shores, missionaries tried to bring order by extolling the positive aspects of the Christian religion. Later, sanctified by their work, they were commemorated in the names of sacred wells, oratories, churches, hermitages and chapels. The first saints were often the martyrs, a popular choice because it was thought that those who died for Christ would be able to intercede in Heaven on behalf of the petitioner. Mainly the saints were Celts, born in Brittany, Ireland and Wales. They were often canonised purely because they founded a church, although some were credited with miraculous powers. Assuming some of the druidic functions of the bards and seers, their influence slowly grew. Many previously pagan holy wells and other sacred natural places were renamed after a saint who was linked in some way to the place.

The site of St Michael's Church is very similar to places chosen in other parts of Britain by these hermit saints. This lovely grassy area overlooking the sea would seem to offer everything a contemplative hermit would require. Conjecture does play a part here, for no physical evidence has been found in the church of early times other than that of Saxon. During renovations to the tower in 1994, a window was revealed and it was realised that most of the tower was originally Saxon, with some later Norman embellishments. The porch of the church comprises the remains of the Norman nave and in the baptistery is an impressive Norman arch leading into the early 16th-century nave. This was the chancel arch of the old Norman church, which supplanted most of the Saxon building. This fine church has some beautiful stained-glass windows and has been sensitively restored with various period features remaining. The oak pulpit and west gallery were carved in Jacobean times. The late 13th-century Brussels tapestry hanging on the north wall of the nave portrays the marriage of Henry VII and Elizabeth of York. It was found behind a false plaster wall in an ancient house in Somerset. The Rev. Edward Peek purchased it for £20 and subsequently gave the tapestry to the church in 1886.

A short walk from the church is the Leper's Well. On the hill above was a friary, founded in 1246. The monks were of the Order of the Blessed Virgin Mary of Mount Carmel, known also as White Friars after the colour of their habits. Carmelite monks were a mendicant order, relying on alms and indulgences in line with their vow of poverty. They founded a lepers' hospital at Lyme towards the end of the 13th century that was built around the well. This hospital cared for many of the local people who had contracted leprosy or other serious skin complaints. In 1336 a lepers' chapel was built, the chapel of the Blessed Virgin and Holy Spirit. Lepers were not allowed to worship in public churches for fear of contaminating fellow worshippers.

The well basin is mediaeval but the structure surrounding it is 19th century. The well house backs on to a high old wall which could be a remnant of the friary. By drinking the water and washing afflicted parts of the body, holy wells were thought to cure a variety of ills. Whether this particular well was seen as having specific healing energies by the friars or was just a useful supply of water, the sound of the stream and stillness of the well create an atmosphere of peace to the benefit of all who visit.

MAPPERTON
The Posy Tree and Plague Burial

OS maps: Explorer 117, or Landranger 193 and 194

Grid refs: Parking SY504998, Posy Tree SY497996, South Warren Hill SY485993

Directions: Approx. 1 mile east of Beaminster on the B3163 turn south to Mapperton. It is not obvious, but just past Mapperton Gardens is a small car park (with parking for a small fee) at the Old School/Village Hall on your right. Continue on foot along the lane for approx. 500 m to the second footpath on the right, where the Posy Tree once stood at the beginning of a rough track, Dead Man's Lane. Take this track and after approx. 500 m at the top of the hill bear left (the valley further to the left was where the white deer were seen). Keep following the bridleway signs until a gate leads to the head of a valley with South Warren Hill on the left and North Warren Hill on the right. Go left towards the grove of trees atop South Warren Hill. The footpath leads down to Melplash but the road that runs through the village is narrow and busy and so it is advisable to turn back and retrace your steps. This is one of the longer walks in this book at about 4 km (2½ miles), but the views are rewarding.

Nearby refreshments: Sawmill Café, Mapperton House; Half Moon Inn, Melplash

The name 'Posy Tree' is redolent of summer and flowers, with an image perhaps of little bunches, 'posies', being lovingly tied to leafy branches. The truth of this tree, an ancient pollarded sycamore, is not of whimsy and floral excess but of dread and darkness. The Posy Tree was so named because of the habit of carrying posies to ward off infection and mask the stench of death (as in the nursery rhyme *Ring a ring o' roses*). Posies were worn around the neck, on wrists and in a little bag over the heart, known as heart bags. Sweet-smelling herbs, such as rosemary, and rose petals were mixed with laurel, camphor, aloes and peppermint leaves. Posies probably festooned the tree as a protective device and a warning at the beginning of the route of the dead.

The Posy Tree was found on the outskirts of Mapperton, at the crossroads of a lane and footpath known as Dead Man's Lane. Sadly, the tree was felled in the latter months of 2011. Health and Safety reasons were cited, as the tree was dead and unstable. The photograph which illustrates this chapter is probably the last one taken before it was felled.

Dead Man's Lane is an old Corpse Way where the bodies of the dead were taken from Mapperton to Netherbury churchyard for burial. Mapperton church was built on rock and it was the tradition for the villagers of Mapperton to bury their dead in the graveyard of their neighbouring village. When, in 1582, about 80 Mapperton souls fell victim to the bubonic plague (Black Death), the inhabitants of Netherbury, armed with staves, barred the grisly burial procession

from reaching its final destination, as they were frightened the disease would be carried into their village on the corpses. The old track passed by South Warren Hill and this eminence was chosen as the most suitable alternative for burial. A pit was dug on the side of the hill near the top and the bodies were interred. A grove of trees covers the site, in a somewhat protective capacity, but occasionally human bones are found, dug up by burrowing animals.

The Black Death first came to Britain in 1348. It was borne on ships coming from Bordeaux to Weymouth and spread swiftly, approximately 50% of the British rural population succumbing to it. In its first year, it raged through Dorset with a grim and terrible determination, carrying many of the villagers of Mapperton in its foetid wake. This might have been when the first Posy Tree was planted, thought to have been an oak. In 1582 the second large-scale inundation of the disease took hold, with most of the villagers succumbing, and 1665 was the last infection within the village. The 17th-century parish records do not mention South Warren Hill as the place of burial for the latter tragedy and it is thought that this hill was only used as a place of interment once, in 1582.

Part of Dead Man's Lane shows an early cobbled surface, possibly mediaeval in origin. There is the feeling that this is a very ancient lane and also a rather strange one. The first time I walked along its length, I felt it lived up to its name as a lane of death. I was at the beginning stretch, now part of the Jubilee Trail, and after a hundred yards I saw a dead magpie lying at the side of the track. Soon after seeing the little corpse I turned left onto the part of the track known as Dead Man's Lane and it wasn't long before I saw a dead rat lying on the cobbled surface. Closer to the beginning of South Warren Hill, near a copse I saw, in quick succession, a freshly dead cock pheasant without a mark on it and the desiccated remains of three other animals.

As the lane progresses towards the hill it becomes a little overgrown but still passable. Before the hill, to the south, is a beautiful downland valley and it was in this valley that I saw a most magical sight. As I was walking in early summer, I glanced back into this large blind valley and saw in the distance a small herd of animals resting in the sunshine – possibly calves or maybe Alpaca, as a few farmers in this part of Dorset keep them. Two of the animals were white, so Alpaca was a probability. I continued on my way, not wanting to disturb them but intending to take a closer look on my return. On the way back I walked closer to the group, to ascertain what they were. Sensing me, they got to their feet and started to run, with the long leaping strides of deer. They cleared the fence at the far edge of the field and disappeared into an area of copse and rough scrub.

They were Roe deer, gathered together in a group of about seven, which is fairly unusual in itself and made doubly so by having two white members in their herd, one snowy white, the other, in all probability the yearling descendant, slightly less pristine. A white deer is the stuff of legend and myth. The Celtic view was that a white deer was a messenger from the Otherworld and this sacred beast should never be killed. A white deer in folklore suggests the route to discovery of some kind, indicating the entrances to magical realms and places of knowledge. The sighting of the deer close to the burial site seemed like a benediction to the souls whose bodies had been interred under the trees at the top of the hill. Lonely and little visited, all kin probably long gone, the validation of their existence lies now with the wild things. From the hilltop one can see Netherbury and its church. Burial on South Warren Hill ensured that even though the plague victims were refused permission to be interred in the graveyard at Netherbury, it was at least within sight and gave sanctification from afar.

Dating from the 1540s, nearby Mapperton Manor stood firm during the plague years though wreathed in sadness. The familiar workaday bustle of the surrounding villages, once merry, succumbed one by one into deathly quiet and the great house stood alone. The empty cottages were eventually pulled down and the old village all but disappeared. Of the original Tudor manor house only the gabled north wing remains. In the 1660s Richard Brodrepp instigated changes to the building, erecting a 17th-century hall range on the site of the 16th-century hall and in the mid-18th century a later Richard Brodrepp gave a classical front to the house and made internal changes in keeping with the times.

Adjacent to the house is All Saints' Church, which dates from the 12th century. Of that period the only visible remains are the font, which is placed on a modern base, and possibly the south doorway and east window. The southwest tower and blocked west doorway date from the 15th century, whilst the pulpit and choir stalls are 17th century. The nave was rebuilt in 1704 and in 1846 the church was once again extensively repaired. The little church contains some fascinating examples of early stained glass, and other items of interest include a fine 18th-century monument to Richard Brodrepp and his children, an Italian altar crucifix *circa* 1700 and a 15th-century Tuscan framed stucco bas-relief of the Virgin and Child. The gardens that flank the house range from formal Italianate to luxuriant plantings and there is a lovely stream-enhanced wild garden. They are open through most of the summer months and the house more occasionally. The house, church and gardens are some of the most exquisite in Dorset and well repay a visit.

MELBURY BUBB
A Curious Font and Tiny Church

OS maps: Explorer 117 or Landranger 194

Grid ref: Church ST596066

Directions: From the A37 approx. 11 miles north of Dorchester, take the turning east to Batcombe, then immediately left signposted Melbury Bubb. Follow this narrow lane under the railway, then turn left at Redford. At Hell Corner turn left to Melbury Bubb and park near the end of this no-through road. For St Edwold's Church, return to Hell Corner and turn left. Take the second left signposted Stockwood and Dorchester, go over the railway line, and after ¾ mile park near the turn to Church Farm on your left. Walk down the farm drive and St Edwold's church is tucked away behind the farmhouse.

Nearby refreshments: Wriggles Farm Produce Shop and Chetnole Inn, Chetnole; Rest and Welcome Inn, Melbury Osmund; Acorn Inn, Evershot

'Rime Intrinsica, Fontmell Magna, Sturminster Newton and Melbury Bubb ...' is the opening line of the much-loved poem *Dorset* by John Betjeman, which evokes much that is quintessential about the Dorset countryside.

Melbury Bubb is a remote hamlet consisting of a Jacobean manor house, farm and few cottages. The small settlement is in the lea of the old beacon hill of Bubb Down which lies behind the church. The River Wriggle rises in the southwest of the parish, eventually joining the Yeo River. The hamlet is named after a local Saxon landowner, Bubba. There is only one lane leading in and out, so no through-traffic disturbs the calm here.

However, the peace was shattered in November 1694 by a violent murder on Bubb Down. The victim was a farmer named Thomas Baker of Bublawns Farm. He owned a number of packhorses and ran a business carrying goods from Evershot to Bristol, which resulted in him carrying large sums of money. One night he was returning along the old drove that led across the hill to his farm with a bag full of money after a successful few days, when he was startled by two assailants. They pulled the protesting farmer from his cart and killed him by crushing his skull with a rock. The robbery turned out to be a bungled affair as the money had been placed in two saddlebags flung over the flanks of one of the horses. The terrified creature, along with its fellows, swiftly bolted towards the Baker family farm and the warmth and comfort of its stable.

It took a long time for the robbers to be apprehended, but they were finally convicted 7 years later, victims of their own stupidity. As they were drinking at the Acorn Inn in Evershot, the alcohol loosened their tongues and they began arguing about the killing. The landlord overheard their talk and informed the authorities who swiftly arrived and took them to the village lockup. Dorchester Assizes was their next destination, where they were duly convicted of murder and sentenced to death. They were enclosed in an iron cage hung from a tree next to an old chalk pit on Bubb Down, close to where the murder had been committed, and there left to die of starvation and exposure. The old drove became known as Murderer's Lane and the place where the felons were gibbeted became the Gibbet Pit. Thomas Baker's phantom horse and cart carrying his body back to the farm reputably haunts Murderer's Lane. Dark and foggy November evenings seem to be the optimum time for sightings.

Thomas Baker's headstone can be found in the churchyard of the village church of St Mary the Virgin. There are also some interesting old table tombs that date from the 17th century. Opposite the church door is the oldest one, erected in 1622 for Alexander Buckler. The worn base of the mediaeval village cross stands southeast of the porch, a relic of the times when these crosses were plentiful in Dorset. Preaching crosses often predated the churches that eventually stood on or near the same site. In Anglo-Saxon times there were more of these standing crosses than churches on many of the lordly estates.

The foundations of the church are 13th century, but it was rebuilt in 1474 under the auspices of Rector Walter Bokeler, whose initials are carved on some of the shields on the tower. Apart from the tower, the body of the present church dates from 1854, when it was heavily restored. Some of the early glass has been retained, as has the font, which is Anglo-Saxon. This font is a fascinating piece of carving, thought to be a hollowed-out base of an 11th-century cross, although it is difficult to equate Christianity with the subject matter that constitutes the carvings on its bowl. The larger animals have been variously described as a stag biting a serpent whose coils interlace the feet of the other animals. They comprise a lion, panther, horse with paws rather than hooves and wolf. The smaller creatures are equally odd. There is something rather like a lizard, plus a bizarre dog, and three indeterminate creatures with copiously looped and knotted tails. To complete the oddities of this strange font, the carvings have been turned upside down, as if a parallel world is represented, the Underworld perhaps, the place of magic and strange beings.

The Anglo-Saxon world continued the animist view of the Celts. Nothing was totally straightforward and life was underpinned by a shadowy world that contained all the old nuances of a tribal culture steeped in what we would call superstition. Meaning was ascribed to the ways of animals and birds, some of which has been handed down to us today. Many still know the old riddle of the magpies – one for sorrow, two for joy, three for a girl, four for a boy. The powers of nature were found within a tenuous world that worked within the realm of imagination.

Melbury Bubb lies at the end of Hell Lane, a name also found in North Chideock. The sinister-sounding name could be derived from Helis, the sun

god. This small hamlet lying at the foot of Bubb Down has not only a natural unspoilt beauty but also the strange wonders found in and around the church, and so richly rewards a visit.

Only a few hundred metres away, on the northwest slopes of Bubb Down in the hamlet of Stockwood and next to Church Farm, is Dorset's smallest church. It is also the only Dorset church dedicated to St Edwold, who had a cell, a tiny building of utmost simplicity, at Cerne Abbas and possibly one here at Stockwood. This small church is thought to have Anglo-Saxon origins but was rebuilt in the 15th century, with further additions in the 17th and late 19th centuries. As this church is so close, it is worth seeking out.

MORCOMBELAKE
Untamed Hardown Hill

OS maps: Explorer 116 or Landranger 193

Grid refs: Ryall road parking SY402942, Hardown Hill SY405944

Directions: There are various routes up to Hardown Hill, but parking is generally very limited around Morecombelake. The shortest and easiest route is to park in the layby/ on the verge ¼ mile along the Ryall road, on the east of the hill. Walk approx. 200 m further along the lane and a path on the left leads directly to the hill. Alternatively park in Shipp Knapp (see next entry), for a more strenuous uphill walk.

Nearby refreshments: Farm Shop and Moores Biscuits, Morcombelake; Five Bells Inn, Whitchurch Canonicorum

I have included this hill because it is one of the few in the area that still retains most of its wild covering of flowers, shrubs and small trees. In summer the air is heavy with the scent of heather and herbs and in the background, the subtle, yet pervasive coconut tang of yellow gorse flowers flavours the air with a whisper of the Tropics. When the heather is blooming, Hardown is carpeted with pink-purple flowers and, seen from a distance, the hill stands apart from the greens of its surroundings and shines as a beacon to high moorland memories. At 207 m (673 ft) it offers wonderful views of Langdon Hill and the landward side of Golden Cap to the south, and Lewesdon Hill and Pilsdon Pen to the north.

Two Bronze Age tumuli lie on the hilltop. Only a small proportion of people were buried in mounds; obviously such people were important to the tribe and

grave goods can sometimes give a clue to their identity. Near Upton Lovell in Wiltshire, an early Bronze Age barrow was excavated, revealing the remains of a shaman. He wore a cloak on which 36 bone points had been sewn and a necklace of similar bone points. By his knees the four large boar tusks that were found may have decorated a pouch. Four axe heads lay beside him, the most impressive being a black stone battle-axe. Also found was a circular polished clouded stone, milky in colour, which was placed on his chest and may have been used for scrying. Scrying employs objects such as a clouded stone or crystal ball in order to gaze with the eyes unfocused so that images can arise which are seen with the 'inner eye'. There were four small cups hollowed out from split flint nodules, plus a collection of stones from many different areas at his feet. The smith was regarded as having magical transformative powers, and a set of hammers and grinding stones were amongst the grave goods, suggesting that smithcraft had been practised by the deceased. Faint traces of gold remained on the grinding stones so it is probable that this talented individual was also a goldsmith.

The shaman is still a powerful figure today, working within the Siberian, Korean, South American and Native American tribal cultures, to name a few. In Britain and Europe, shamanism was a living force whose seeds were sown in the Ice Age. The Palaeolithic cave paintings of Les Trois-Frères in Ariege, France, show two examples of a shaman, one with a bird-headed staff and another horned and dancing. Shamanism existed in Europe for thousands of years until, with the advent of Christianity and the accompanying lessening of belief in the spiritual animation of nature, the shaman metamorphosed into the cunning man and wise woman, becoming more secretive and solitary.

Today there is a burgeoning re-interest in shamanism in Britain and the USA, a legacy of the heady hippy days of the 1960s. People wanted a spiritual outlook other than that provided by Christianity. Eastern spirituality, such as Buddhism, started to attract adherents and Native American peoples, with their earth-orientated religion and way of life, were seen as having wisdom that non-Native Americans wanted a share in. The Native American medicine man was basically a shaman and shamanism began to earn some probity when academics started to take an interest. The shaman is the bridge between two worlds. Communication is realised when a state of trance is achieved via dance, drumming, meditative stillness or natural hallucinogens. The abode of spirits is then accessed, a place generally known in Britain as the Otherworld. That all aspects of nature share a kinship is the guiding tenet of shamanism. Everything vibrates with life and can be communicated with – from flowers, trees, rivers, pools and rocks, to the sun, moon and stars; these are all animate and have personal identities. The knowledge that shamans have with the inner world of nature is used to help members of the tribe. The healing ceremonies performed are with the understanding that human beings are intrinsically part of the natural order, not separate. Because of their understanding and sensitivity to the energies of the land, shamans find the sacred places and 'power spots', utilising them for vision and healing. These places can be caves, hills, pools or a gnarled and twisted ancient grove of trees – anywhere there is 'numen', the inexpressible sense of 'something'. A shaman would give back something to these centres, sending a prayer for the people's wellbeing and leaving an offering as a reciprocal gift.

We do not know who was buried on Hardown Hill, except that they had been singled out for special treatment. One barrow was disturbed by a later intrusion of burials dating between AD 450 and 550. The bodies were buried a few feet below the surface, with their heads to the west. Nine spears and a brooch were also excavated, indicating that one of the skeletons was that of a woman. Maybe she also owned the pebble with a natural hole bored through it, also found in the tomb, an object known in rural areas as a witch's stone and valued as a good luck charm. Dorset fishermen used to hang the 'hag stone' upon a rope at the stern of the boat as a protective charm.

Opening up a burial mound for later use was sometimes done as a mark of respect, linking present-day dead with the dead of the past, for it was thought and was probably true that barrow burial was only given as a mark of respect to a special member of the tribe. The bloodline of that tribe very possibly can still be found in the few local people who have remained in the area, remnants of an unbroken line of succession. This re-using of prehistoric burial mounds ceased in the 7th century.

In summer when the air is scented and balmy, looking west through the Scots pines to the sea beyond Charmouth is a view that brings a feeling and sense of the Mediterranean. Hardown seems a forgotten hill somehow, not as popular as the nearby, larger, coastal Stonebarrow Hill, which is a beautiful sweeping eminence but one that in comparison possibly lacks the singular intimacy and wildness of Hardown Hill.

MORCOMBELAKE and WHITCHURCH CANONICORUM
A Holy Well and Pilgrim Church

OS maps: Explorer 116 or Landranger 193

Grid refs: Ship Knapp SY399939, Church SY397954

Directions: From the A35 at the western end of Morcombelake, turn south into Ship Knapp lane and park considerately. Approx. 200 m up the lane, take the footpath on the left through a gate into a field. The well/spring is adjacent to the path, surrounded by a small fence and only 400 m from the lane. To visit St Candida's Church, drive back to the A35, turn left, then immediately right to Whitchurch Canonicorum. After 1 mile, turn right at the crossroads and the church is just past Gassons Lane. There is a small car park tucked away to the left.

Nearby refreshments: Farm Shop and Moores Biscuits on the A35 in Morecombelake; Five Bells Inn, Whitchurch Canonicorum

In a field to the south of Morcombelake is a holy well, a simple square water-filled stone basin. This spring is dedicated to St Wite, thought to have been a 9th-century Anglo-Saxon hermitess or holy woman living in quiet contemplation near the well site. But sadly, much as the virtues of contemplation sooth and nourish the soul, the outside world can still violently intrude. Nearby Charmouth was used as a landing point by the Danes who came as pirates, looting and causing havoc. In 831 a huge number landed, slaughtering many of the local populace before being driven away by the Saxon King Egbert. It is assumed that St Wite could have lost her life in this raid.

For hundreds of years the well has been renowned for its healing properties, particularly for eye complaints. 'Eye wells' are often dual purpose – helping, via bathing, physical eye complaints and also having the ability to be used for vision of a more subtle kind, to open the 'inner eye', for spiritual growth, vision and prophecy. Our early ancestors felt that water was

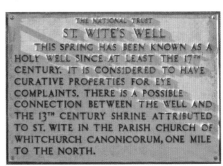

a visible manifestation of the life force. Pools and springs were also seen as entrances to the spirit world, places of soul, of life, and many were ascribed to a god or goddess. Later these wells were rededicated to Christian saints, an example being that the Celtic goddess Bride became St Bridget. This could have also happened at the well here, for it is possible that St Wite's well was formerly

Painting 7: The plain and simple well of St Wite is situated in a small fenced-off enclosure in a meadow, by the footpath. Sometimes the greater the sanctity, the lesser the ornament, testament to the veneration in which this well used to be held.

a pre-Saxon pagan cult site, as Wite could also mean Gwen, a goddess still known in Wales.

St Wite is connected to the church of St Candida and the Holy Cross at Whitchurch Canonicorum, about 1 mile north. The church has early foundations, being built by King Alfred the Great as a dedication to St Wite in the latter part of the 9th century when the church was known as Hwitan Circian. It was largely demolished in the 12th century by monks from the Abbey at St Wandrille in Normandy and a Norman church replaced the old Saxon building. The new church was formally dedicated to St Wite around 1200 and was further extended in the 13th century. Some time between then and 1500 it was rededicated to St Candida, the Latinised form of St Wite, and the appellation 'Holy Cross' was added in the late 15th century.

In the Middle Ages this church was an important place of pilgrimage and was referred to as 'the Cathedral of the Vale' for, apart from Westminster Abbey, it is probably the only post-Reformation church to contain a saint's shrine and relics, to which petitions are still made. Pilgrims would come from afar, gaining refreshment in the 14th-century Shave Cross Inn, situated beside one of the pilgrim routes that afforded safe travel through the wild and wooded Marshwood Vale. The church still bears the marks of incised votive crosses on the east jam of the inner south door, made during pilgrimage as marks of veneration. There are other interesting carvings on the outer wall of the church, including one of St Candida. To the west of the porch is a carved, inverted two-handled flagon, typical of the 12th century and thought to represent the Holy Grail. Though difficult to see, on the tower are carvings of a boat and axe and, to the right of the small window, an axe and adze. These carvings possibly come from the early Saxon church and have been incorporated into the later structure. They seem to be alluding to the Danes who killed St Wite.

The main object of interest inside the church is perhaps the 14th-century stone shrine, placed on a 13th-century base. There are three oval openings (mandorla) in the coffin where people would place written petitions or insert their afflicted limbs in the hope that proximity to the relics of the saint would induce a cure. Interestingly, the tomb became split by subsidence and, during restoration work in 1900, a casket was discovered. Inscribed upon it were the words *Hic Reqesct Relique Sce Wite*. When opened, it was seen to contain the bones of a small woman aged around 40 years old. A thighbone was missing but was rediscovered in 1910 in Lambeth Palace, labelled 'the thigh bone of St Candida'. Over the centuries there have been many stories of people being healed of their ills here. In the past, crutches and sticks were left in the church as proof of the authenticity of this shrine. The powers of healing move in mysterious ways and if belief is there, a cure often follows.

Whitchurch Canonicorum has an interesting history. In Jacobean times a friend of Sir Walter Raleigh, Sir George Somers, lived here at Berne Manor. As an experienced naval officer, he was commanded by King James I to help set up a colony in Virginia. Encountering torrential storms on the journey, his ship foundered on an uninhabited Caribbean island. This island was named Bermuda and became a possession of the English Crown. In appreciation, Sir George was made Admiral of Virginia. He later died on Bermuda and his heart was brought back to Whitchurch for burial.

An old custom, now died out, was to place oak branches around Whitchurch Canonicorum on Oak-apple Day (29 May) to commemorate the anniversary of the Restoration. The boughs were cut before dawn and the church tower and crossroads were decorated first. Then, to the ringing of the church bells, branches were put over the doorways of the cottages, houses and farms in and around the village.

PORTLAND
Church Ope Cove

OS maps: Explorer OL15 or Landranger 194

Grid refs: Parking SY695713, Cove SY697711

Directions: Take the A354 onto Portland, up past the Portland Heights Hotel and through Easton. At the end of wide Wakeham Avenue you pass the Portland Museum on your left, then on the bend there is a car park on the right. Walk back past the museum and down Church Ope Lane. After passing under Rufus Castle, enjoy the view before taking the steep steps down to the Cove. After exploring the Cove, start back up the steps, but turn left at the sign for ruined St Andrew's Church. Continue up through picturesque woods below Pennsylvania Castle to directly opposite the car park. The woods have a mix of steps and slopes, and can be slippery.

Nearby refreshments: Portland Museum; Easton

Deadman's Bay, aptly named as it is the site of numerous shipwrecks, lies to the west of Portland, and a jagged row of rocks known as the Shambles, also lethal to shipping, lies to the east. Portland had good sea defences against invasion but sadly many innocent vessels have broken up on the rocks, including passenger boats, inevitably leading to large losses of life. The hinterland of Chesil Beach is said to contain the graves of some of the hundreds of victims of these wrecks. Washed up on the shore by violent gale-swept waves, the bodies were buried often where they lay. Church Ope Cove has also been the recipient of this maritime carnage, but its main attraction is its beauty, both of location and beach, lying as it does below the ruins of St Andrew's Church and Rufus Castle. Many centuries ago a mermaid was reputedly seen washed up on the shore here, witnessed by churchgoers.

The son of William the Conqueror, William Rufus, probably constructed Rufus Castle in around AD 1100. The castle is unusual for two reasons. The first is the building's shape, which is that of an irregular pentagram, unique in Britain. Second, the skill of the stonemasons was used to good effect in that the walls were built without the use of mortar, a building technique that was a rarity in Norman times. Over the centuries the castle suffered damage, the first occasion being around 1140 during feuding between Empress Matilda and King Steven. There were also attacks from France at various times, leading to major rebuilding in around 1450.

Also above the Cove is the sadly ruinous St Andrew's Church, which used to be the parish church of Portland and the main place of worship for Portlanders. It has probable Saxon origins and the site has yielded an Iron Age coin and shards of Romano-British pottery. There are still a few traces left of the Norman

church which was built in 1100 under the auspices of an order of Benedictine monks. However, during the 14th and early 15th centuries French marauders landing in the Cove attacked the church, eventually causing so much damage that a partial reconstruction had to be carried out in 1475. Parts of this later mediaeval building remain, but the structure was not as sturdy and slowly the mortar crumbled and the stones fell. This decay, coupled with the small size of the building that was becoming inadequate for the burgeoning population, led to its abandonment in the mid-18th century. Cliff erosion was also a contributing factor, the Southwell landslip of 1675 leading to loss of part of the churchyard. The church became increasingly ruinous, particularly as much of the stone was used in the building of the replacement parish church, St George's at Reforne, which was completed in 1756. Some finely carved stones from the church can be seen in Portland Museum.

The churchyard has some interesting headstones. On one there is an unusual carved head, and on another a skull and crossbones. This has given rise to the legend that the grave is that of a pirate. It is more likely that the skull and crossbones is a *momento mori*, an image of death as a salutary reminder that our time on earth is brief and death comes to all.

In the private grounds of Pennsylvania Castle, hidden behind brambles, are the remnants of John Penn's Bath. John Penn was the grandson of the founder of Pennsylvania. In 1800 King George III gave him some land on the Isle of Portland on which he built Pennsylvania Castle, designed by James Wyatt, a well-known architect of the time. King George had made sea bathing popular as a healthy pastime so Penn had a bath carved out of the rock on land halfway between his house and the sea at Church Ope Cove. Penn was unpopular with

the islanders as he had enclosed the land on which Rufus Castle and the church were built and locals now had no right of access. When the bath was completed the Court Leet decided that it had been built on common land and a heavy rent was charged for Penn to use it. Penn abandoned his bath in disgust, but his servants were delighted as they no longer had the tedious task of carrying buckets of seawater up to the bath.

Church Ope Cove has had very little disturbance to interfere with its natural beauty. The slight intrusion of the scattered beach huts is tempered by the quaintness of the wee gardens that surround them. Piles of stones make up the rough walls of these little patches of pebbles and plants. An old well is situated at the bottom of the steps that lead to the beach. The history of this well is uncertain; it could be a holy well, its dedication long forgotten, or it could be just a simple provider of water.

PORTLAND
Ancient Culverwell

OS maps: Explorer OL15 or Landranger 194

Grid refs: Portland Bill parking SY677685, Southwell parking SY689701, Culverwell Mesolithic site SY685693

Directions: Take the A354 onto Portland, up past the Portland Heights Hotel and follow signs to Southwell. Culverwell is on your right adjacent to the road, mid-way between Southwell and Portland Bill. When open there is parking on the site for up to 15 cars, otherwise park in Southwell (free) or at Portland Bill. The site is open to visitors from 2–5 pm from May to the end of August, on the first Sunday of the month, plus Bank Holiday Mondays. Other than these times the site can be opened by special arrangement by calling Susann Palmer on 01305 861576.

Nearby refreshments: Lobster Pot Café and Pulpit Inn, Portland Bill; Eight Kings Pub, Southwell

Portland is a limestone peninsular slightly over 4 miles long and nearly 2 miles wide. It rises to about 135 m (approx. 400 ft) at the highest point and is an unusual landscape feature known as a tied island, connected to the mainland by Chesil Beach. There is a luminous type of light engendered on Portland that is created when a narrow spit of land is surrounded by sea. The light reflected from the waves together with the whiteness of rock that constitutes most of the land combine to create a translucency that bears a strange and subtle beauty.

Portland has been a Royal Manor since Saxon times, a situation giving unique rights and privileges. The islanders have their own governing body created by the Saxons, the Court Leet, and are able to create some of their own governances and laws. The relative isolation in which the people lived and the fact that marriages tended to be between island families created a strong feeling of kinship, identity and respect for their unique tract of land.

Years ago, sheep farming and fishing were the main livelihoods, the native Portland sheep attracting fame for the quality of their meat. Some of the villages still have the wide streets associated with driving the huge flocks. Wakeham near Easton is an example of this and the wide main street, lined with plain grey stone cottages, seems to epitomise the

particular quaintness that people find so intriguing about parts of Portland, the quality of an honest simplicity combined with solidarity and strength. The islanders' lives changed in the 16th century when Inigo Jones discovered both the quantity and the quality of the rock at Portland and used it for building the great Banqueting Room at Whitehall. The valuable limestone that makes up the bulk of the land, known as Portland stone, had been utilised in a small way since Roman times, but after Jones's approval, demand hugely increased and quarrying became the main industry on the island. The particular stone found here, known for its density and whiteness, has been used for some of the finest buildings in Britain, such as St Paul's Cathedral, the Houses of Parliament and National Gallery.

The 19th century saw a huge increase in quarrying activity, and a new influx of trade and commerce with the rest of Britain brought an infusion of strangers to Portland. As island identity began to be diluted, it brought with it a lessening of closeness to the land and huge quarries began to eat out the heart of Portland. Many places of special beauty and character disappeared, along with countless prehistoric sites.

There still survives, now in very few places, early evidence of occupation in prehistoric times. Near Portland Bill is an ancient well (Culverwell), tucked away amongst a spread of small trees and bushes. The well consists of a spring lined by stone slabs and in summer wild watercress can be found here.

The abundant fresh water is probably the reason for the nearby Mesolithic settlement being sited here. Dating from about 6000 BC (the Middle Stone Age), this site is of national importance. It was discovered in 1966 by the sharp eyes of local archaeologist Susann Palmer. As she was walking in a field that had recently been ploughed she noticed large quantities of mollusc shells, typical debris found around prehistoric habitations. A year later, a small team of volunteers led by Palmer started to excavate the area, an excavation that continued on a part-time basis over the next 30 years. This initial modest find lead to the discovery of the remains of one of the oldest settlements in England, which was probably inhabited all the year round. [See Palmer (1999) for details.]

The main features of the site comprise a natural gully running north to south down the slope of a hill with smaller gullies in the south. There is a large shell midden, the shells being mainly that of limpets, dog whelks and periwinkles. On top of this midden is a floor of limestone slabs, besides which is a smaller paved area and to the south is a low wall forming a windbreak. There are a series of hearths, a pit and a number of features with a ritual aspect, an example being a large triangular stone incorporated into the floor. Next to the stone is a large beach cobble and underneath is a stone-lined hole containing a pierced scallop shell, axe and round pebble planted on its edge in the midden material – possibly a foundation deposit, a gesture aimed at ensuring strength to the homestead, or these might have been offerings to a particular deity. Other possible ritual items that have been found are collections of uniform round pebbles and the remains of a small semicircular feature by the wall. The floor is a simple structure composed of Portland stone and provides the earliest evidence of the use of this stone for building purposes. Many chert tools have also been excavated and a lesser quantity of flint. It is thought that between 15 and 30 people lived here in three or four small huts over a period of 10–20 years.

PORTLAND
King Barrow

OS maps: Explorer OL15 or Landranger 193

Grid refs: Parking SY690731, King Barrow SY691728

Directions: Take the A354 onto Portland and proceed uphill to the Portland Heights Hotel. Turn left at the roundabout in front of the hotel for free parking and a panoramic view over Portland Harbour and Weymouth. Walk along Yeates Road behind the hotel and the signed entrance to the Dorset Wildlife Trust King Barrow Nature Reserve is on your left, with an information board.

Nearby refreshments: Portland Heights Hotel and White Stones Café, Easton

At one time there were many Bronze Age barrows or burial mounds on Portland, but most have disappeared due to quarrying, building and farming. King Barrow was thought to be the largest and was still visible in the late 19th century. Now it remains in name only, giving its title to the Dorset Wildlife Trust Nature Reserve conceived in the small former quarry that was the cause of the destruction of the barrow. Here also are underground 'beehive' chambers, thought to have been excavated in Iron Age times for the storing of grain but possibly similar to the fogous of Cornwall, which were believed to have had a ritual use. These structures were dug from solid rock and formed of flat stones. They have a small opening at the top and were up to 3 m high. In them have been found traces of grain and pottery, sling stones and domestic animal bones.

Standing stones have also gone. The Victorians named a group of stones in nearby Easton Lane 'The Frolic'. They formed a stone circle, thought to be a druid temple, in the Grove (evocatively named) on the site of what is now the Young Offenders Institution. Folklore tells of human sacrifices at this site and superstition surrounds this part of the island. Between Southwell and the Bill a large standing stone once stood, giving its name to the area known as Long Stone Ope. There are other place-names such as Bridge Stone and Butts Stone, indicative of ancient lost stones in the area of Southwell. 'Beehive' chambers or 'dene holes' have been found in this locality and excavation has unearthed Roman sarcophagi carved out of the local stone. Only one burial mound now remains on Portland, Mound Oel, which is in a private garden in Chiswell and is difficult to find as it is tucked away between buildings. It is most visible at the southern end of Clements Lane. Gary Biltcliffe's book *The Spirit of Portland: Revelations of a Sacred Isle* has much to say about these sacred stones and places on Portland.

King Barrow Nature Reserve has been allowed to regenerate naturally and, in the relative peace and seclusion it offers, wildflowers such as Horseshoe Vetch, Kidney Vetch and Autumn Gentian grow freely. Adonis and Chalkhill Blue butterflies can be seen, as well as birds such as Whitethroats, Linnets, Meadow Pipit and, at dusk, the elusive Little Owl.

POWERSTOCK
Castle Hill and Powerstock Common

OS maps: Explorer 117 or Landranger 194

Grid refs: Castle Hill SY521959, Powerstock Common DWT car park SY547974

Directions: From Bridport take the A3066 north. On the northern outskirts of Bradpole turn right and follow the signs to Mangerton Mill and Powerstock. Approx. 1 mile after West Milton turn left to Powerstock village. Park near the church junction or ask at the Three Horseshoes pub. Walk approx. 400 m along King's Lane (below the church) and take the footpath on the right. Fork left along the stream and the path takes you around the base of Castle Hill. You can walk approx. ½ mile further along King's Lane and access Powerstock Common on the corner at Whetley Farm. By car, drive up King's Lane to Eggardon Hill, turn left and after approx. 2 miles you can use the Dorset Wildlife Trust car park on the left.

Nearby refreshments: Three Horseshoes, Powerstock; Marquis of Lorne, Nettlecombe

Powerstock used to be called Poorstock in Mediaeval times. The nearby hamlets of North and South Poorton retain the old spelling. Powerstock Castle, on a site known as Castle Hill, is traditionally thought to have originated as a winter palace for the grandson of Alfred the Great, King Athelstan of Wessex. Later there was a Norman motte and bailey here. At the beginning of the 13th century, King John exchanged lands with Robert de Newburgh and acquired Poorstock Manor. Once in his ownership, he built or rebuilt a large hunting lodge on the site. He only stayed five times between 1205 and 1213. After King John died in 1216, the castle passed to his son Henry III who also used the place infrequently and who, after 3 years, passed the tenancy to his Sergeant-at-Arms, Thomas Gorges, a member of the family who owned both Shipton Gorge and Litton Cheney, and thence to Gorge's family and other tenants. In 1306, Edward I gave Poorstock and the castle to his daughter Mary, who was a nun. She was thought not to have used the castle, which although tenanted through the years gradually fell into disrepair and ruin. Over time people have found carved stones and roof tiles, but none of the structure is now visible, any vestiges being hidden under the turf.

A wooded path leads through trees to the lower slopes of the castle site. The forlorn remains of the castle now consist of banks and rough mounds. Small trees and shrubs are scattered over the area and it is hard to distinguish any features that might give a shape to the ruins, such as walls or foundations. The castle has stood empty for longer than it was occupied and a wistful feeling of loneliness pervades the place. The situation was carefully chosen, both defensively and

aesthetically. Anyone approaching could be clearly observed, as all views from the parapets were unobstructed. Sited within the lea of mighty Eggardon Hill with the primeval fastness of Powerstock Common in the northeast, Castle Hill holds its own, neither overly dominant nor insignificant. It stands as a small wooded jewel, subtle and unimposing yet with a presence worthy of attention.

Powerstock Common is an accessible natural wilderness, similar in ethos to nearby Kingcombe Meadows, but with a more sylvan quality and less tamed. Here wild boar that are probable escapees from some farm secretly lead their lives. They have now covertly returned to an area where centuries ago they used to roam. When a native animal becomes extinct, something is lost from the soul of both the land and the national identity. Wild boar were one of the sacred totem animals of the British Isles. Our ancestors linked them with the goddess, the female principle of life, and because of the large litters the sows produced they signified fecundity. As the sows protect their young with a

fearsome ferocity, the wild boar also signified the berserker quality of maternal protectionism. Great boars of supernatural origin feature in legend and folk tales, sometimes as protectors of wisdom, sometimes as a monstrous test of valour.

The landscape here has managed to escape being intensively farmed and is probably little changed since mediaeval times. The area has kept its natural integrity and has a rare obliviousness to human ways. Yes, there is some human interference here; there are the remains of a disused railway line and a small amount of woodland management, but neither is enough to displace the overall feeling, which is one of a simple burgeoning joy. Wild places, untrammelled by human overfamiliarity, offer presentiments of what life would be like if we lived a little closer to where the natural world is allowed to flourish. Powerstock Common is a valuable resource to show us that wilderness is still with us.

As you sit on the hillside
or lie prone under the trees of the forest,
or sprawl wet-legged by a mountain stream,
the great door that does not look like a door, opens.

Stephen Graham

SHIPTON GORGE
Cult of the Head and Liminal Crossroads

OS maps: Explorer OL15, or Landranger 193 and 194

Grid refs: St Catherine's Cross SY496907, Church SY498916, Shipton Hill SY508922

Directions: Approx. 2 miles east of Bridport on the A35, turn south to Shipton Gorge. There is easy parking and a great view of Shipton Hill from the church. From here walk to the crossroads at the eastern end of the village. Turn left (north). After 200 m, on the right is a lone cottage and the adjacent sunken footpath (Bonhole Lane) leads up Shipton Hill. However, if you can find parking it is a much shorter and easier walk from near Shipton Hill Farm (on the west side) or Higher Sturthill Farm (east side). St Catherine's Cross is south of Shipton Gorge on the road to Burton Bradstock. There is no landmark or sign at this crossroads, but the adjacent house is called by the same name.

Nearby refreshments: New Inn, Shipton Gorge; Anchor Inn, Three Horseshoes and Hive Beach Café, Burton Bradstock

Shipton Hill is an early Iron Age hillfort that has also been used as a beacon hill. The hill is an unusual square shape, somewhat like an upturned boat, though the single rampart and ditch at the base are hard to discern amongst the gorse and small trees and bushes.

Two Iron Age Celtic cult objects, a pair of carved stone heads (now in the Dorset County Museum), were found in a bank close to Shipton Gorge in 1958. Objects such as these were regarded as talismans in mediaeval times and later and were thought to bring strength and good luck to the buildings and walls in which they were deposited. It is a distinct possibility that the original site of these heads was the settlement at Shipton Hill. The Celts followed the cult of the head; the heads of enemies were taken in battle and kept as trophies in order to obtain the power of the enemy. Skulls would be impaled on poles and displayed at the gateway of the fort. It was thought that the head was the repository of the soul and was therefore an object of great power. It stood for divinity because it was seen as containing the essence of being and also had the power of healing and prophecy.

The power of the head is expressed in the *Mabinogion*, a Welsh book of mythic literature. It contains a story about a crowned king of Britain, Bran. He was known also as Bran the Blessed or Bendigeid Vran, of divine origin, being the son of the god Llyr. In a battle with Matholwych, King of Ireland, Bran was mortally wounded with a poisoned spear. Knowing he was dying, he commanded his head to be struck off and carried to the White Mount (the White Tower of London) and buried with his face towards France. Before this deed was done, Bran told the seven men who had escaped the battle slaughter:

And you will be a long time upon the road. In Harddlech (Harlech) you will be feasting seven years and the birds of Rhiannon singing unto you. And the head will be as pleasant company to you as ever it was at its best when it was on me. And at Gwales in Penfro you will be fourscore years; and until you open the door towards Aber Henfelen, the side facing Cornwall, you may bide there, and the head with you uncorrupted. But from the time that you have opened that door, you may not bide there: make for London to bury the head.

Eventually the head reached the White Mount and when it was buried the deed was known as one of the Three Happy Concealments, 'for no plague would ever come across the sea to this Island as long as the head was in that concealment'. The head of Bran is seen as a talisman guarding the fertility of the land and warding off the image and actuality of the Wasteland.

A Bronze Age tumulus lies on the banks of the smaller Hammiton Hill just to the south. Whether there were any barrows at Shipton is now difficult to assess. Possibly the low mound under the Ordnance Survey trig point on the top of the hill is the remains of a barrow. Normally there was reverence accorded to a previous culture's religious sites by Iron Age people and earlier burial mounds were left in situ.

It is always interesting to wonder why particular places were chosen for burial or other ritual purposes. Quite often the tops of hills were chosen because they marked the extent of a particular tribe's territory and a prominent barrow placed on the top was a boundary marker. Other sites remain open to speculation. The Chinese have a name for the currents of energy that run through the land; they call them *lung mei* or dragon lines, and *feng-shui* practitioners are able to recognise sites that would be propitious for different usages, such as building a house or erecting a temple. In Europe there were probably similar people who were sensitive to the energies of the land, the druids perhaps, who would advise on places suitable for a stone circle, standing stone or burial. Vestiges of this knowledge remain in the wilder more untouched places in Britain.

Shipton Gorge is mentioned in the *Domesday Book* and was under ownership of the de Gorges family in the 13th century. The village was originally named in Saxon times *Sepetona*, meaning sheep-farm. In the 11th century, Shipton formed part of the estate held by Thomas Maureward and was renamed Shipton Maureward, a name that lasted nearly two centuries until the de Gorges assumed proprietary rights, giving their name to the village that we know today. The old manor house, known as Court House, used to be sited to the west of the church but nothing now remains, although

Painting 8: The flower-strewn path up Shipton Hill. Often the journey to a place is as meaningful and beautiful as the place itself.

the land is still known as Court Field.

Like many old villages, Shipton had its share of practices now regarded as superstitious. At the beginning of the 20th century a chimney sweep was sweeping the chimney of an old cottage in the village and, having reason to go up into the large chimney, found an old canvas bag hanging from a cranny in the wall about 3 m from the ground. Inside the bag he found a dry blackened object wrapped in paper. It was a bullock's heart, stuck with thorns and pins. This strange old fetish, one of four that had been found in the neighbourhood, was a charm against the spell of a witch. Under the doctrine of sympathies, the thorns and pins tormented the witch and broke any malefic spell.

Shipton church is dedicated to St Martin and is in a pleasant position on top of a small hill. It is possibly sited near where the ancient chapel of St Laurence used to be, with the 13th-century font a remnant of the older building. The tower dates from around 1400 and is all that remains after the church was

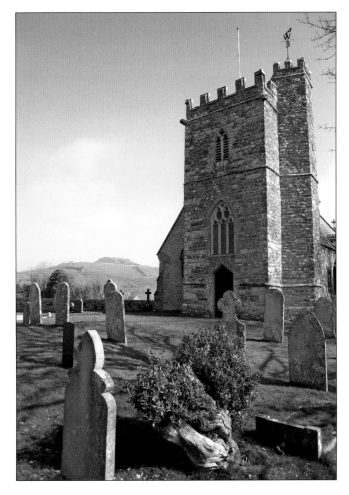

radically rebuilt in 1861. Unusually for a reasonably large community there was no licence to allow burials on the land surrounding the church, and apart from a short period in the 17th century, burials were not permitted here until the mid-19th century. Corpses had to be buried in the churchyard attached to the church at Burton Bradstock, whose ecclesiastical parish included Shipton.

Burton Bradstock is a few miles south of Shipton and the route is arduous as there are steep hills and boggy valleys. To break the journey, corpses would be left overnight in the now long-gone Chapel of Ease dedicated to St Catherine. There is a crossroads here and the place is named St Catherine's Cross in memory of the old chapel. This is reputedly a very haunted site, hosting a variety of strange visitants. On certain nights a spectral coach and horses clatter by, accompanied by a headless Black Dog. Crossroads are amongst places known as 'liminal', areas that are confluences or meeting places of different elements, such as bridges and shorelines. Features such as these are thought of as portals, allowing ingress between the physical dimension and the Otherworld.

In 1999, a man cycling past St Catherine's Cross noticed panic-stricken cows wheeling and milling in an adjoining field. He saw a strange large black animal running fast near the cattle. The exertions of cycling had caused sweat to drip into his eyes, so he quickly wiped them. When he looked again, the black creature had disappeared. Whether it was one of the large mystery cats that many people have seen in West Dorset or the ghostly Black Dog said to haunt the area, there was certainly something that spooked the cattle. There are aspects of life that defy easy categorisation and the message of the irrational is that it opens the door to experience rather than explanation.

STOKE ABBOTT
Waddon Hill and a Lion Spring

OS maps: Explorer 116 or Landranger 193

Grid refs: Parking ST455008, Waterspout ST453007

Directions: Take the B3163 west from Beaminster, then (opposite the school) turn left to Stoke Abbott. On entering the village, look for a row of cottages on the left. Park along the road near here and take the footpath on the right to Chart Knolle. On approaching Chart Knolle House take the left footpath along the northern flanks of Waddon Hill, with its Roman fort remains, up to Stoke Knapp Farm (at the B3162). From the farm, take the sunken lane down towards Stoke Abbott, but after just 300 m pause at the footpath on your left for views of the fort. Take this footpath, along the south side of Waddon Hill, back to Stoke Abbott. To find the trough and waterspout, turn right along the lane, bear left at Manor Farm, and the well is 100 m on the right. The church is a further 100 m on your left.

Nearby refreshments: New Inn, Stoke Abbott; Beaminster; Broadwindsor

Stoke Abbott is a picturesque settlement, protected by a circle of hills, with relatively few new houses and a good mix of old buildings. Manor Farm is a fine example of a grand manorial farmhouse dating from the 16th century. It lies in the lee of the hills, protected yet not overshadowed, for it is a building of character, benevolently dominating this corner of the village.

Villages such as this often have a ghost story or two to tell. A hundred years or so ago, John Symonds Udal, a barrister, learned folklorist and historian, was walking with Major Groves of Bowood along a track that led over the fields. At a certain place, the Major pointed out that this was where a phantom coach-and-four had been seen on various occasions. This track from Bowood to Stoke Abbott still exists and is a lonely old way over the hills. On a full moonlit night, when bats are flying and the air is still, the rumble of wheels and thudding of galloping hooves, signifying the approaching coach and its ghostly occupants, would be enough warning for anyone to get quickly out of the way. The coach and horses is a classic ghostly sighting, of which there are a few in Dorset including one at Kingston Russell, where the driver and horses are headless.

At the foot of the hollow lane that climbs from Stoke Abbott to Broadwindsor is a trough and waterspout. The two springs that come out of the hillside, filling the trough and cascading from the spout with a constant supply of water, were probably instrumental in the first founding of a settlement here. Village people still drew their water from the bubbling supply until 1961 when piped water supplanted that of the spring. Some people preferred the natural spring water for cooking and drinking and only used the piped water for bathing and

Painting 9: The lion-head water spout is one of the best-known features of Stoke Abbott. The water from the spring creates verdant growth.

washing clothes. Passing horses still drink from the trough, a square stone basin commissioned by a local man, Richard Symes, and dated 1752. The carved stone lion's head drinking spout replaces an earlier one and dates from 1953, commemorating the Coronation of Queen Elizabeth II.

Stoke Abbott church is dedicated to St Mary the Virgin and the building is thought to be on a Saxon site, although no traces of an earlier building remain. The earliest fabric of the church, a small Norman window, dates back to the 12th century. The church was restored and enlarged in 1878 but various mediaeval parts remain, including a 13th-century chancel, a 14th-century archway in the south porch, a 15th-century tower and various 15th-century windows. The font is of exceptional interest, dating from the late 12th century. The cover, of unknown date, is wooden,

embellished with extremely skilled and beautiful iron decorative work, and the bowl and stem, carved from a single rock, depict eight heads around the bowl, four men and four women. They possibly represent Noah, his wife and sons, each with a wife.

The name Waddon Hill probably comes from the Old English for wheat or possibly from Woden, chief god of the Anglo-Saxons and the ancestor god to kings. He was multifaceted, being the god of death, battle and wisdom, the shaman wizard of knowledge and discoverer of runes and poetry. Another name for him was Grim, and Grim's Ditch is a long banked Anglo-Saxon defensive structure, fragments of which are found in the south of England. Grim means hooded and the archetypal image of Woden is of a tall one-eyed hooded being, wise beyond all knowing, wearing a long black cloak, with two ravens as his sentinels. One can see why 'grim' has passed down to us as an adjective with rather sinister connotations.

Waddon Hill rises between Broadwindsor and Stoke Abbott. It has a distinctive flat top and is the only hill in the district that is the site of a Roman fort. The fort was built on order of Vespasian in around AD 50 and was probably an advance position, soldiers being garrisoned here during the initial stages of the Roman campaign. Quarrying in the late 19th century uncovered coins and pottery with, more importantly, a finely wrought iron scabbard with inlay of gold and silver, now on show in Bridport Museum. Later excavations discovered that the structure of the fort was mainly of wood, slotted into the limestone core of the hill. It is thought it lasted for roughly a decade before being dismantled and abandoned.

The Roman campaign was a drawn-out show of strength, aimed at subduing the local tribes. The Durotriges reigned over this part of Dorset and were responsible for many Iron-Age hillforts in the area. These forts acted as both protection from the Romans and a show of strength against the Devon-based Dumnonii. However, the Romans had the skills and manpower to outwit most of those they came in conflict with and both the Durotriges and Dumnonii eventually suffered defeat. The fort is on the west of the hill, where a good lookout could be afforded over the Marshwood Vale in the south and across Somerset to the Mendips and Blackdown Hills in the north. Soldiers would have been based here during attacks on the fort and settlement on nearby Pilsdon Pen. Roman forts normally had an area set aside for a temple to a god or goddess and as a bronze bust of Mercury was found here several decades ago, this deity was likely to be the presiding god of this encampment.

Mercury has various traits and functions, the main being that of messenger of the gods. Other attributions are that of a psychopomp or guider of souls to the Underworld. In this he has links with Woden, who as leader of the Wild Hunt also rounded up lost souls and took them to the proving grounds of Asgard. The ghostly coach and horses haunting the lane between Stoke Abbott and Bowood is an echo of this. According to Julius Caesar, Mercury was the

main Roman god venerated in Britain. As an intermediary between the gods and humans, Mercury's proclamations, received by seers through trance, gave added veracity to battle plans and campaigns and strength to the premise of actions sanctified by the gods.

The view from Waddon Hill in its southern extremity takes in the sea along the Jurassic Coast. As the coastal cliffs erode and slip, the dust of millions of years comes to light and brings forth prisoners; stone shadows of strange creatures. But not only the coast plays host to fossils. Waddon has an interesting secret, for ammonites, found in the shallow seas of the Pleistocene era, have been found on the heights of this hill too, especially in quarried areas where the rock has been broken and disturbed.

As an endnote to this chapter, I draw attention to a very special man who lies buried in St Mary's churchyard, the renowned mystic and sage John Michell, who died in 2009. He was a prolific writer on the subtle energies of earth mysteries, expounding on the idea of a celestial landscape laid out across the British Isles. One of his initial impetuses was an interest in ley lines, sparked by the work of Alfred Watkins. In the 1920s, Watkins was the first to discover ley lines and published a book on his findings, *The Old Straight Track*. Watkins had a vision whilst standing on a hill near Hereford. He saw straight lines between churches, hilltop forts, barrows, standing stones and other similar places. All these sites were linked by what Watkins considered were ancient track-ways. In the late 1960s Michell started his writing career with two seminal books, *The Flying Saucer Vision* in 1967 and *View Over Atlantis* in 1969. Of the two, the latter expounded in detail his view that ley lines were more than just track-ways, but were in fact currents of energy and magnetism, vivifying the land in tune with the heavens. The Hermetic maxim 'as above, so below' is a succinct illustration of this primal idea. He lies buried close to the large old yew tree.

SYNDERFORD RIVER
Romantic Waters

OS maps: Explorer 116 or Landranger 193

Grid refs: Access points at Halscombe Bridge ST392014, Synderford ST382037, Shedrick Bridge ST378049

Directions: The southern end of this 5-km (3-mile) path starts at Halscombe Bridge, the northern end being Winsham. Halscombe Bridge and Synderford make good vantage points for viewing by car or bike.

Nearby refreshments: Winsham; Thornecombe; Squirrel Inn, Laymore; Bottle Inn, Marshwood

The Synderford River rises on the lower slopes of Pilsdon Pen near Attisham Farm and joins the River Axe just below Winsham. This small river has a footpath running alongside most of its length, which allows for an intimate wander beside its softly moving waters.

The southern end of this path starts at Halscombe Bridge near Racedown, a Georgian house made famous by the fact that William Wordsworth and his sister Dorothy lived there for 2 years. They rented the house from John Frederick Pinney, son of John Pinney of Bettiscombe, a wealthy local merchant who felt his social standing might be increased by contact with the Wordsworths. The house suited Wordsworth and while he worked on *The Borderers – A Tragedy*, daily walks with Dorothy supplemented his studies. It was Dorothy, working diligently in the garden, who was, one summer day, surprised by Samuel Coleridge, who had walked all the way from Nether Stowey in Somerset. The end of the Classical and beginning of the Romantic Movement was seeded by the fusion of ideas between the two poets and their friends.

The Romantic Movement recognised the importance of the idea of 'spirit of place' (*genius loci*), seeing it as a reality infused with extraordinary inspirational qualities. Writers and artists are allowed a certain freedom and licence to express their ideas about the outré and arcane and the landscape became a template, fuelling the Movement's outpourings. Under the Romantic vision, the union of nature and spirit was envisioned as a benign influence on the human soul, one that could bring about ultimate harmony. Wordsworth would undoubtedly have walked along Synderford River. He would have found inspiration in the unceasing flow and eddy and movement of light and dark. Trees overhang much of the river and cast their shade over shallows and depths. This is an accessible river through much of its length, with deep pools here and there, deep enough to harbour a large trout or two.

Each river has its own character according to the geology and contours of the

land. The rivers rolling lazily through buttercup-strewn water meadows are very different to the wild mountain torrents of the uplands. Large rivers such as the Thames and Severn catch the bounty of smaller rivers that flow into them, increasing their girth and majesty with each in-pouring of different waters. These small rivers are like a choir, adding their voices to the general song that culminates in a grand aria on meeting the sea.

Various cultures see rivers as frontiers, giving access to another realm and acting as a vehicle for rites of passage. Baptism in rivers is an initiation, releasing the person from their old life. The Pre-Raphaelite painter John Everett Millais created the memorable image of Ophelia floating in her death swoon down the flower-festooned river, leaving her past life behind. This ties in with the Greek legend of the River Lethe, the River of Forgetfulness that dissolves previous identity so that one is born again, with no recollection of previous lives.

The Celts recognised water as the first principle and source of all life. The river represents the primal waters, analogous to the breaking of the waters as a precursor to birth. As primal waters give life they also perform that duty in death, affording a passage for the newly dead to the Land of the Dead, the Summerland or Hades. The River Styx is an example. Stonehenge is linked, via the avenue, a ceremonial route, to the Avon, a Celtic word meaning river. Recent excavations by archaeologist Mike Parker Pearson have unearthed traces of a small bluestone circle at the side of the River Avon where the avenue ends. This is thought to have ritual significance, the river being seen as a possible route for the dead, conveying the remains to their final resting place. Another ceremonial route leads from the nearby large henge monument of Durrington to the mortuary temple of Woodhenge and thence to another part of the River Avon. The river seems to be acting as a vehicle connecting the two avenues, as a sort of spirit highway.

Sabrina, the Latin name for the goddess of the River Severn (known as *Hafren* in Welsh), and *Tamesis*, the old Brythonic name for the Thames, meaning 'dark water', are old names for two of our major rivers. The larger rivers were thought to have a deity attached. The Scottish River Clyde is named after *Clota*, the Divine Cleanser, known in legend as the 'Hag of the Ford', a foreteller of death if her ghastly figure was seen washing, over and over again, a pile of blood-stained clothes at the river's bank. Anthropomorphic application of human traits onto animate and inanimate objects is derided by science yet has a long history within human culture. It is part of the idea that there is no separation between humanity and the natural world. Rocks, stones, the tiny voices of the sands, all are seen, along with the larger landscape, as having a type of consciousness and life. When there is a powerful force of nature, such as a river, that can have both malefic (flooding) and beneficial influences on life, there is a tendency to attempt mitigation of the seeming randomness of the effects brought by such a powerful energy. Everything is animate to various degrees and the core of this animation comes from the interior life of the world, what we could call the 'soul'. The powers that have a huge influence on life and death, such as the weather, the aforesaid rivers, the oceans, plants, animals and disease, are rendered approachable by the naming process of attribution to a goddess or god.

The early Celtic Christianity of Britain recognised the power and influence of the natural world as part of God's creation, and a whole and beautiful part at that. But when the power of the church moved to Rome, attitudes changed and nature was seen as base and unsanctified. The credo brought into play at that time, that of man having dominion over the animals, led to a lack of sympathy and understanding of the natural world and animal kingdom, and a seemingly irrevocable estrangement was the result. The modern Green movement and renewed interest in paganism have begun to redress the balance.

Moving fresh waters, such as rivers and streams, are living manifestations of a special force, seen by many people as sacred. The essence of this sacred quality comes from the admixture of minerals and vegetative properties and, more especially, ethereal qualities, influenced by the moon's phases, of the

springs that are the birth of the river above ground. This admixture of different types of elements, both physical and numinous, creates what is seen as the regenerative powers that streams and rivers possess. So the little River Synderford, on its short journey to the River Axe, spills out life-enriching qualities of a profound subtlety, and if one cares to look deeper into its reflective grace, there can be seen there the pure poetry of endless ebb and flow.

TOLLER FRATRUM
The Knights Hospitallers

OS maps: Explorer 117 or Landranger 194

Grid refs: Church and manor house SY578972

Directions: Approx. ½ mile west of Maiden Newton on the A356 turn south to Toller Fratrum. Just before the lane peters out, turn right up the drive to Little Toller Farm and Manor House. Park near the gate to the church (on the right). The adjacent manor house and refectory buildings are private and cannot be entered without permission.

Nearby refreshments: Maiden Newton

Toller is derived from the Celtic *tol* meaning hollow and *dwr* (eventually becoming 'ler') meaning stream, so *toller* means a stream in a valley. *Toller Fratrum* means 'toller or brook of the Brothers' and the Brothers in question were those of the Knights Hospitallers, also known as the Knights of St John, an order formed during the Crusades. In this they were similar to the Knights Templar excepting that the Hospitallers, who admittedly had a martial aspect, were a healing order, mainly inclined to provide medical care and hospitality, of a spare kind, to journeying pilgrims.

The Knights Hospitallers have a long history. The Blessed Gerard founded them in 1113 and his successor Raymond du Pay de Provence established the first Hospitaller infirmary near the Church of the Holy Sepulchre in Jerusalem. At first the Hospitallers cared for pilgrims in Jerusalem, but as the order grew it was able to provide travelling pilgrims with an armed escort. In this way they were similar to the Knights Templar. The Hospitallers and Knights Templar, who were formed later in 1119, became a powerful Christian force. By the mid-12th century the order had two distinct branches, the military brothers and those who cared for the sick. Privileges were granted by the Papacy; the order was exempt from all authority apart from the Pope; it was allowed its own religious buildings; and it paid no tithes. Some Knights Hospitallers were based in Toller Fratrum from the 12th century and probably lasted until the Reformation. They would have cared for the health of pilgrims travelling in the vicinity. Some of these pilgrims would have been travelling to Whitchurch Canonicorum to visit the shrine of St Wite and to other pilgrimage sites in the area such as Glastonbury.

The hamlet of Toller Fratrum is situated on a hillside overlooking the River Hooke. It consists of a few cottages, a farm and a manor house that was built on the site of the old monastery by John Samways in 1540 and later added to by Sir Thomas Fulford in the 17th century. The main part of the house dates from this time and is a typical example of the large houses of that period. Twisted stone chimneys loom over pinnacles carved into strange heraldic beasts. One of the carvings depicts an ape holding a mirror. Athelhampton Hall near Puddletown has a similar carving of an ape, suggestive of the unsettling family motto *Whoever looks at Martyn's Ape, Martyn's Ape shall look at him.* Athelhampton Hall has many ghosts, one being that of a monkey that was accidentally walled up, to die a lonely death of starvation.

The building at the side of Toller Fratrum manor house, now used as a barn, used to be the monks' refectory. Above a window is a worn stone carving of a monk eating a loaf of bread. The mellow stone barn is in a ruinous state of repair, with much of the thatch fallen in and the beams rotted. The ecclesiastical nature of this long building, typical in shape and size to many of the simple mediaeval refectories, has been subjected to the requirements of farming life and now hardly exists. Only one or two of the original windows, panes broken and most glass gone, reveal by their shape the original purpose of this old building.

Adjacent to the back of the barn is an interesting small church built on a promontory overlooking the River Hooke and unusually dedicated to St Basil. Only two other English churches are dedicated to him, as St Basil is better known in the Coptic churches of the East. Known as Basil the Great, he is linked to

Damascus and would have been known to those fighting in the Crusades. St Basil was a 1st-century saint who was born in Caesarea. He was an inspired scholar and theologian whose writings on the Holy Spirit form part of the basis of Coptic and Roman Catholic theology. He is the patron saint of Russia, amongst other countries, and is honoured as one of the greatest saints of the Greek Orthodox liturgy. The Knights Hospitallers probably brought back knowledge of St Basil to Britain.

The church dates from the 12th century. It has suffered a large amount of Victorian 'improvement' but still retains simplicity, being of a basic rectangular shape with a bell cote at the west end. Either side of the door are two simple stone heads. These are similar to Celtic stone heads and possibly they were unearthed and attached to the church to sanctify their pagan origins. The interior of the church is pleasant but plain; it does, however, contain two exceptional objects. One is the Anglo-Saxon/early Norman font, which is slightly older than the font at Melbury Bubb and shares some of its oddness, with its strange monster carvings and head motives, possibly linking with the heads either side of the entrance door. Near the altar is another interesting relic, a 12th-century broken piece of carved stone depicting Mary Magdalene washing Christ's feet with her tears. This fragment of simple carving has a sweet quality of devotion, both in the poignant image of an act of love and in the effort that has been shown in the care of the carving.

TOLLER PORCORUM
Churchyard Megaliths

OS maps: Explorer 117 or Landranger 194

Grid ref: Village hall parking SY562979

Directions: Two miles west of Maiden Newton on the A356, turn left to Toller Porcorum. On entering the village, take the second right (School Lane), then left into Church Mead and park in the village hall car park behind the church. The two large stones are either side of the main churchyard entrance.

Nearby refreshments: Kingcombe Centre, Toller Porcorum; Maiden Newton

Toller Porcorum, known in Saxon times as Swynestolre, lies in the valley of the River Hooke. *Toller* means 'a stream in a valley' and *porcus* is Latin for pig. Domestic pigs roamed the woods here, put out in autumn to feast on acorns and beechnuts. Wild boar were once hunted in the extensive woodland that edges much of the village. They were hunted to extinction in Britain, the last one killed in the mid-17th century. However, escapees from farms have settled in various parts of the country and they have now returned to the area, a small population ranging between Powerstock, Toller Porcorum and Hooke.

The church of St Andrew and St Peter is situated on a roughly circular raised site in the middle of the village. Records date back to 1235, but history implies that priests served here for many years prior to the beginning of records. The tower dates from the 13th century. The font is particularly interesting as it is part of a Roman altar. Whether there was a Roman temple on the site prior to the first church being built or whether the altarpiece came from another Roman site in the area is a matter for conjecture. The font is decorated at the corners

with rams' heads, a motif recognised by both Christian and pagan religions. In the former, the ram represents the Lamb of God, and in the latter, possibly Ares, a tyrannical Greek god of war, similar to the Roman Mars. The astrological Aries is a zodiac sign symbolised by a ram's head, so there are various choices that can be made about the iconography of this unusual font.

The situation of the church gives it a highly visible position in the village. Sites similar to this were popular in pre-Christian times as places of celebration and worship and it is possible that prior to the church being built, there was a stone circle here. Some years ago two megaliths were discovered whilst rebuilding segments of the collapsed surrounding wall. They had been incorporated into the wall and possibly left in situ and the wall built around them. This raises a few questions – were they part of a stone circle, the other stones being lost, or were the monoliths a couple of standing stones that were already in place on the hillock? The stones are similar in type to the stone circle near Kingston Russell as they seem to be in their natural shape and are the same sort of oolitic stone, a limestone derivative.

At Knowlton, near Wimborne in East Dorset, there is a fascinating conjunction of a church within a pagan site, demonstrating the Christianisation of a sacred place of earlier times. Inside the raised bank of the henge monument are the ruined remains of a Norman church. It is probable that a stone circle stood inside the henge, the stones of which were used in the building of the church. A survey discovered two barrow cemeteries to the north and south of the henge, and to the east is the largest round barrow in Dorset, the Great Barrow. In all, there are the traces of at least four circular structures in the area, so it would seem that Knowlton, in use from 2500–1700 BC, was an important spiritual and ritual site. The ruinous 12th-century church at Knowlton preserves most of its tower and still has its old altar in the remains of the chancel. The Black Death of 1348 wiped out most of the villagers and so the church lost much of its congregation, until it was finally abandoned in the 18th century. The henge and church have the unearthly reputation of being the haunt of demons and witches.

It is unlikely that Toller Porcorum contains hidden remains on the scale of Knowlton, but the hill on which the church stands is significant because it is a small conical hill. This is the sort of landscape feature that was often chosen in prehistoric times as the site for some sort of edifice – a monolith, circle of stones or barrow. Thus there is a distinct possibility that the church here was, like Knowlton, built on an earlier place of pagan worship. If so, with different emphasis and guises, there has been a spiritual practice here since the earliest of times and it continues still. The fey hill has subtly and unobtrusively hosted worship over the ages as a little beacon on the edge of the darkling forest.

UPLYME
An Ancient Yew and Black Dog

OS maps: Explorer 116 or Landranger 193

Grid ref: Church and parking SY325934

Directions: Take the B3165 northwest out of Lyme Regis for 2 miles until you come to Uplyme. Turn right after the petrol station into Cooks Mead, then right again, past the school, and park at the church.

Nearby refreshments: Talbot Arms, Uplyme; Lyme Regis and Raymonds Hill

Although technically just over the border into Devon, the postcode is Dorchester and I have included Uplyme in this book because of two interesting features/stories. Uplyme is a small village on the edge of Lyme Regis. It was first recorded in AD 740 when King Cynewulf of Wessex ceded the village to Glastonbury Abbey. In 1850 the remains of a Romano-British villa were discovered nearby and it is probable that there was a settlement in this area before Saxon times.

There is an interesting legend attached to Uplyme, that of a ghostly Black Dog. Until 1994 there was even a Black Dog Inn. The story goes that in the 19th century a family was walking up Haye Lane (formerly known as Dog Lane) in the evening when they saw a little black dog padding towards them. As it got closer, the dog became larger and larger, becoming an enormous black cloud, which enveloped them. The cloud moved on, leaving fear and bewilderment in its wake. Local people are still reluctant to walk the lane after dusk, as there have been other strange sightings in the vicinity, such as that of a puma-type big cat seen in a field by the River Lim by a couple in 2004. Another story tells of a local man who was regularly haunted in his own home by a Black Dog. He got so fed up with the 'ghost' that he chased it with a pole into an attic. The dog disappeared through the ceiling but his pole disturbed a box of gold and silver coins which subsequently fell out of the roof. Haye Lane leads to this house.

The church is dedicated to St Peter and St Paul and dates back to the 9th century, though it is now a Victorian restoration apart from a 14th-century tower. In the churchyard a venerable yew grows on a mound to the west of the entrance – an enormous tree, probably more ancient than the church itself and possibly over a thousand years old. It has grown to a huge stature, casting a dark numinous presence over this piece of hillside for a very long time. Of huge girth, this ancient yew is one of very few of a similar age in Dorset.

In the Welsh language, many words signifying awareness, knowledge and writing are related to the word for wood, *wydd.* Three examples are *cywydd* ('revelation'), *gwyddon* ('wise man') and *derwydd* ('druid'). The tree also

symbolised the cosmos in some cultures, such as early Scandinavian, which venerated the strange Yggdrasil, the World Tree of the Viking sagas. Notable trees such as Herne's Oak in Richmond Park, London, situated next to a hollow known as Fairy Dell, are seen by 'sensitives' as the outward manifestation of the spiritual qualities of a place. The druid bards had 'trees of inspiration', and this tradition has been revived at Caerwys in North Wales where a sycamore was planted in the mid-20th century as the tree of inspiration for the Eisteddfod (an annual competitive festival of Welsh poets and musicians).

The yew tree has an interesting reputation and history. Both druids and Christians regarded it as a symbol for everlasting life due to the great age it can attain. The yew also grows in a unique way because after many hundreds of years it tends to become hollow in the middle, its trunk rotting over time, leaving the lower branches to eventually take root in the ground. They become new trunks encircling the old central trunk, the whole eventually growing as one. This new growth arising from the old has seemed to many to be a symbol of death and rebirth.

In Irish mythology the yew is one of the five sacred trees brought from the Otherworld and it was also seen as a magical tree in pagan Britain. Thought of as a guardian of the cycles of death and rebirth, transformation and reincarnation, the yew stands as a gateway between the mortal world and that which lies beyond. In Ogham (the cryptic alphabet inspired by trees, supposed to have been created by Irish druids as a secret means of communication), the yew is called Idho and is known as a chieftain tree. The Otherworld associations

continued into Christian times where yews have always been associated with churchyards. Churches were often built on places that were sanctified by our pre-Christian ancestors and mostly the inherited yews were left alone. The yew at Uplyme links both the misty past of animated nature and the structured role of Christianity, which tends to render nature comatose. However, there is now an increasing awareness of the importance of regaining our natural roots and links with the land. Our ancestors were not uncouth savages but people who possessed a knowledge and respect for the environment and wildlife that hugely influenced the way they lived. Their lives were more circumspect and intricately meshed with nature. This old tree in the churchyard at Uplyme has a long history that is a living testament to longevity.

WALDITCH
Spinners' Lane and Real Tennis

OS maps: Explorer 116 or Landranger 193

Grid refs: Hyde Tennis Club SY480925, Spinners' Lane (start) SY484927

Directions: Take the A35 east out of Bridport and after only 300 m from the roundabout and petrol station, take the right turn to Walditch. Follow the lane for approx. ½ mile and just after Hyde Barn Cottage is an imposing building on the right housing a real tennis court. A little further on is the church. Towards the far end of the village opposite a house called Landfall is a footpath sign on the right to Shipton Gorge. This footpath is Spinners' Lane.

Nearby refreshments: Bridport

This village close to Bridport owes its original name of Waldyke to its location in the valley of an encompassing curved hill. The hill has a dry-stone wall stretching to Bothenhampton. Somewhere in Walditch is reputed to be a spring, its whereabouts now unknown but possibly in the grounds of the Hyde Nursing Home, where people used to put the water in bottles and use it to heal eye complaints.

In the west of the village is a substantial chapel-like building that houses one of the few (about 27) real or royal tennis courts in the UK. Real tennis is the racquet sport, using cork balls and 27-inch racquets, from which modern tennis derives. The term 'real' was used from the mid-20th century to distinguish from the modern game of tennis. The early game where hands were initially used instead of racquets began in 12th-century France and came to England in the early 15th century, due to the interest of Henry V. Later, Henry VIII further developed the game and in 1530 built a tennis court at Hampton Court, the largest and finest in the country where he played enthusiastically. The court in Walditch is open to the public and you are welcome to take a look inside.

The village church of St Mary was completely rebuilt in 1863. In a Victorian gothic way it is an atmospheric building and repays a visit. Of the mediaeval chapel originally on the site no trace remains.

Spinners' Lane further up the main street is a deeply sunken hollow lane. Two thirds of the way up the hill is generally passable, but the last part is overgrown with brambles and bushes and so the track leaves the old sunken way and rises upwards onto the grassy hillside. Here the openness and light are in marked contrast to the green gloom of the old track. Spinners' Lane gained its name from the flax spinners of Shipton Gorge who used this route to deliver their wares to Bridport. Outworkers spinning the flax grown in the area would travel from outlying villages to the main centres of collection. Resourceful local women who were the main spinners could turn their hands to most things when the need arose and this work provided extra income when farm work was slow.

After about 800 m at the end of the wood, you can turn right to enjoy a circular walk back to Walditch church. The left track to Shipton Gorge strides over the chalk pastureland and becomes part of the old shepherds' ways, legacies of past times when sheep were abundantly reared on the steep scarp slopes covered with species-rich grassland. Expansion of sheep farming in Dorset began in the 14th century. Local sheep were slowly bred to produce, in the 19th century, the Dorset Horn and Dorset Down breeds, both hardy and producing excellent meat.

Historic Spinners' Lane and the downland track to Shipton Gorge are two distinct topographies – the time-forgotten hollow way and the rolling Dorset downs. One is internal, deep, dark and slightly unsettling. The other is external, into the light and heights. Both are valuable together as a balance and counterpoint.

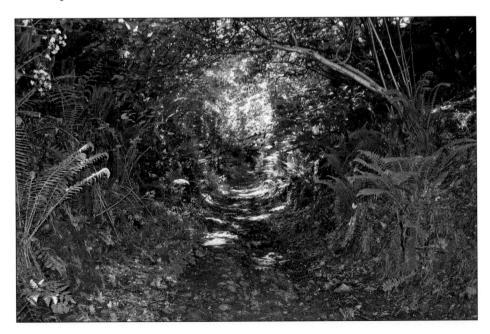

WEST CHELBOROUGH
A Timeless Village

OS maps: Explorer 117 or Landranger 194

Grid ref: Church ST542054

Directions: From Evershot go west on the Beaminster road for approx. 1½ miles and take the second right to Chelborough. After ½ mile turn left at Grexy Cross and West Chelborough is at the end of the lane. Park near the telephone box.

Nearby refreshments: Halstock village stores; Talbot Arms, Benville; Acorn Inn, Evershot

West Chelborough, a seldom-visited village, was the subject of an article written some years ago by Candida Lycett-Green as part of her series 'Unwrecked England' for *The Oldie* magazine. She described the village as a gem, situated in a landscape that reminded her of Tuscany. The same holds good today; this delectable tiny village, more of a hamlet, is still a settlement based around a church and surrounded by land that consists of hills, woods and open undrained pastureland, similar to parts of the Tuscan landscape. The cottages are mainly old former agricultural dwellings and, save for the normal conveniences, unmodernised for the most part. There is a parkland feel to the fields, a generosity of space blessed with a perfect balance of trees and small woods, the turf dotted with wild flowers and grazed mainly by sheep.

The old church is dedicated to St Andrew and has a Norman tub-shaped font, a 17th-century tower and 18th-century chancel. The main body of the building is restored 15th-century Perpendicular style and the walls of the

church are built with local yellow-ochre ham stone. A stone effigy of a mother and child lies inside, commemorating Lady Kymer who died in childbirth. The Kymers were lords of the manor from the 14th to the 17th century. There are also quaint old memorials on the walls, of which one is inscribed:

> *Look here, my friends, behold and see*
> *This house of clay in which I be*
> *Pray do not lament for me,*
> *But scan your own Mortality*
> *For I am here in earth, confind*
> *To leave my little ones behind*
> *As now I be with you shortly must,*
> *Be here with me and lodge in dust*

West Chelborough encapsulates how many small settlements used to be. It lies off the beaten track, somewhat remote yet with enough local people still living in it to keep alive a feeling of continuity and familiarity. There is a sense of cohesion to the place, with the cottages edging the central church and farms providing a living throb of life and movement.

Old track-ways lead out into the surrounding meadows and woods, providing a connection with outlying villages. One track leads to Corscombe a few miles away and another to East Chelborough. If the villagers in the old days wanted something elsewhere they would have walked these paths, but there is a feeling of completeness suggested by West Chelborough that hints that these paths were rarely used.

WEST MILTON
A Hollow Lane and Old Church Tower

OS maps: Explorer 117 or Landranger 194

Grid refs: Parking SY502963, Hollow lane SY503967, Church tower SY503964

Directions: About 1 mile north of Bridport on the A3066, turn right at Gore Cross and follow the signs past Mangerton Mill to West Milton. Park near the bus shelter and proceed on foot up the lane towards Leigh Gate, passing the old church tower. The start of the hollow lane is approx. 500 m on your right, on the brow of the hill. Walk just 300 m up this lane to Beningfield Wood Nature Reserve.

Nearby refreshments: Mangerton Mill Tea Rooms; Three Horseshoes, Powerstock; Marquis of Lorne, Nettlecombe

The hollow lane that travels north from West Milton is ancient and atmospheric and worth exploring. At the beginning its banks rise as high cliff, waning slightly as the lane is ascended. Leading up through trees, this is a real hollow way that has receded below the level of the surrounding countryside – a lane that through centuries of use has become worn away, eroded down to the bedrock, becoming deeper and more tunnel-like.

Hollow way comes from the Anglo-Saxon *hola weg* meaning 'harrowed path' or 'sunken road'. Old route-ways are an understudied and underappreciated component of our historic landscape and Dorset is rich in these old ways – the drove roads, pilgrim paths and routes to the sea that are our archives of the past. Many date from the early Iron Age or even earlier and these sunken labyrinths of wildness, forgotten and underused, are hallowed as well as hollowed. There is a haunting associated with this particular hollow lane. A funeral cortege is said to wind its ghastly way along this age-old track, lighting the dark with a sepulchral glow, seen only by the night creatures.

Returning to the village, after a few hundred yards there is an iron gate and, upon entering, a small churchyard lies somewhat forlorn, denuded of most of its graves but still containing an old yew tree. In the corner of the churchyard is a mediaeval tower, which is all that remains of the Grade II Listed 15th-century church of St Mary Magdalene. This church was demolished and a new church built on the main lane through the village. This was also demolished after less than a hundred years, leaving West Milton with two churchyards but no church. The early graveyard has a charm given by the proximity of the mediaeval tower, adding a fairy-tale quality to its surroundings and a lift to the quiet melancholy that forgotten graves exude. When churches are demolished, which mainly happens because of poor repair, the tower sometimes remains standing and many Victorian churches are built around the old mediaeval tower. The church of St Michael here in West Milton just seemed to fade away. No rebuilding was ever done at this site and the other site in the village held a church for only a short while.

The churchyard has a view along the valley to Powerstock and beyond to Eggardon Hill. The wrought-iron gate at the far end of the churchyard opens on to a path that leads to Powerstock through stream-edged meadows. If the current West Milton villagers felt the desire to attend a church, the nearest one would be at Powerstock, and if they wanted to walk, this would be the route they would probably take, and a fitting prelude to the church service it would provide. To begin one's approach to God by a route that is embellished by beauty provides a taste of grace and a sense of the spiritual immanence in nature.

In Summary

This book contains a personal selection of places that have atmospheres both haunting and engaging – places in tune with the surrounding landscape but also unique and unusual. Whether these are linked with past people and events or have unspoilt qualities that are rare in this current age, they all are subtly rewarding.

I hope you have enjoyed the rambles in this beautiful part of Dorset and made discoveries that, in one way or another, are enriching and enlightening. I also hope I have provided an introduction to some aspects of our countryside that offer a sense of 'soul'. As the Native American Navajo saying goes, 'May you walk in Beauty'. West Dorset proffers beauty in abundance.

Bibliography

Ashley, Harry and Hugh (1984) *The Dorset Village Book*. Countryside Books, Newbury.

Bailey, C.J. (1982) *The Bride Valley*. Dorset Natural History and Archaeological Society, Dorchester.

Best, Rosemary (1970) *Poorstock in Wessex*. Dorset Publishing Company, Bournemouth.

Biltcliffe, Gary (2009) *The Spirit of Portland: Revelations of a Sacred Isle*. Roving Press, Frampton.

Boswell, Barbara (undated) *Leigh. A Dorset Village*. Self-published.

Briggs, Katharine (1967) *The Fairies in Tradition and Literature*. Routledge and Kegan Paul, London.

Colquhoun, Ithell (1955) *The Crying of the Wind*. Peter Owen, London.

Colquhoun, Ithell (1959) *The Living Stones*. Peter Owen, London.

Cooper, Adrian (1998) *Sacred Nature*. Capall Bann, Chieveley.

Creed, Sylvia (1987) *Dorset's Western Vale*. Dorset Publishing Company, Milborne Port.

Crowden, James, and Wright, George (2006) *Dorset Man*. Agre Books, Bridport.

Dacombe, Marianne R. (1951) *Dorset Up Along and Down Along*. Dorset Federation of Women's Institutes, Dorchester.

Doel, Fran and Geoff (2007) *Folklore of Dorset*. Tempus Publishing, Stroud.

Gardiner, Dorothy (1949) *Companion into Dorset*. Methuen, London.

Harpur, Merrily (2008) *Roaring Dorset! Encounters with Big Cats*. Roving Press, Frampton.

Harpur, Patrick (1995) *Daimonic Reality*. Arkana, London.

Harpur, Patrick (2002) *The Philosopher's Secret Fire*. Penguin, London.

Harpur, Patrick (2010) *Complete Guide to the Soul*. Rider, London.

Harte, Jeremy (1986) *Cuckoo Pounds and Singing Barrows*. Dorset Natural History and Archaeological Society, Dorchester.

Harvey, Graham, and Hardman, Charlotte (1996) *Pagan Pathways*. Thorsons, London.

Hutchins, John (1873) *The History and Antiquities of the County of Dorset*, Volume 4. Republished 1973. E.P. Publishing, in collaboration with Dorset County Library, Dorchester.

Jesty, Chris (1986) *A Guide to the West Dorset Countryside*. Dovecote Press, Wimborne.

Jones, Gwyn, and Jones, Thomas (1949) *The Mabinogion*. J.M. Dent and Sons, London.

Jones, Prudence, and Matthews, Caitlin (1990) *Voices from the Circle*. Aquarian Press, London.

Knight, Peter (1996) *Ancient Stones of Dorset*. Power Publications, Ferndown.

Knott, Olive (1954) *More About Dorset*. Longmans at the Friary Press, Dorchester.

Legg, Rodney (1987) *Mysterious Dorset*. Dorset Publishing Company, Wincanton.

Morris, Stuart (1985) *Portland, An Illustrated History*. Dovecote Press, Wimborne.

Newland, Robert J., and North, Mark J. (2002) *Dark Dorset, Tales of Mystery, Wonder and Terror*. Oakmagic Publications, West Rudham.

Omand, Revd Dr W.D. (1969) *Chideock, its Church, its Saints, its Martyrs and its Sinners*. British Publishing Company, Gloucester.

Palmer, S. (1999) *Culverwell Mesolithic Habitation Site, Isle of Portland, Dorset*. Excavation Report and research studies. BAR British Series 287.

Palmer, Susann (1999) *Ancient Portland. Archaeology of the Isle*. S. Palmer.

Ponting, Gerald (2000) *A Walk to Breamore Miz-Mize*. Charlewood Press, Chandler's Ford.

Pulman, George R. (1969) *The Book of the Axe*. Kingsmead Reprints, Bath.

Putnam, Bill (1998) *The Prehistoric Age*. Dovecote Press, Wimborne.

Sadler, Mary and Peter (undated) *Corscombe Through the Ages*. Privately published.

Sharp, Mick (2000) *The Way and the Light*. Aurum Press, London.

Shillitoe, Richard (2009, 2010) *Ithell Colquhoun, Magician Born of Nature*. Self-published.

Swan, James A. (1993) *The Power of Place*. Gateway Books, Wellow, Bath.

Sykes, Homer (1997) *Celtic Britain*. Cassell, London.

Thomas, Keith (1971) *Religion and the Decline of Magic*. Weidenfeld and Nicolson, London.

Treves, Frederick (1906) *Highways and Byways in Dorset*. Macmillan, London.

Warren, Derrick (2004) *Curious Dorset*. The History Press, Stroud.

White, Jim (2003) *Downs, Meadows and Pastures*. Dovecote Press, Wimborne.

Wiltshire, Kathleen (1975) *Wiltshire Folklore*. Compton Russell, Salisbury.

Woodcock, Peter (2000) *This Enchanted Isle*. Gothic Image, Glastonbury.

Websites

Daniel's Knowle Burial Ground (www.rupertwilloughby.co.uk)

Dorset Historic Churches Trust (www.dorsethistoricchurchestrust.co.uk)

Megalithic Portal (www.megalithic.co.uk)

The Sheela Na Gig Project (www.sheelanagig.org)

Dark Dorset (www.darkdorset.co.uk)

Chideock Catholic Church (www.chideockmartyrschurch.org.uk)

The Mythic Imagination: talks, trails and mysteries (www.mythicimagination.info)

Glossary

adze – an axe-like tool with a curved blade set at right angles to the handle and used chiefly for shaping wood

aire – an ancient type of music

Arcadia – an unspoilt harmonious wilderness, home of the Greek god Pan

arcane – known or understood by only a few

barrow – a mound of earth or stones placed over a prehistoric burial site

berserker – one of a band of ancient Norse warriors known for their reckless frenzy

chert – a form of microcrystallite quartz, a tough rock that can be broken to form very sharp edges

combe – probably of Celtic origination (*cwm*) meaning a dale or valley

Coptic – Coptic Orthodox Church, established AD 42 by St Mark and originally based in Egypt

Court Leet – a court of record held once a year in a particular hundred, lordship or manor with jurisdiction over civil matters or petty offences

cursus – a long Neolithic structure of parallel banks with external ditches. Amongst the oldest of prehistoric remains, they are thought to have a ceremonial function. Originally thought to be Roman athletic courses, hence the Latin name

Dumnonii – meaning 'people of the valley', who had territory ranging over Cornwall, Devon and part of Somerset. The roots of the tribe come from the Bronze Age

Durotriges – a Celtic Iron Age tribe based in Dorset, south Wiltshire and south Somerset

excarnation – removing the flesh from the bones by natural means such as leaving the bodies on platforms to be scavenged by birds or by cutting the flesh from the bones

fae – another name for a fairy. Also someone who can see into the world of the fairies

'familiar' – a supernatural entity taking various guises, normally animal, and assisting witches and cunning folk in their practise of magic

fastness – a wild and uncultivated area

fogous – associated with Cornish Iron Age settlements. From the Cornish *ogo* meaning cave. Purpose unknown, could be refuges, storage chambers or ritual/ceremonial places

Hermetic – having to do with the occult sciences, especially alchemy and magic

imp – a mischievous type of fairy

ley line – a current of energy flowing through the land which has beneficial effects

lias – a type of sedimentary rock

liturgy – a proscribed form or set of forms for public religious worship

malefic – having or exerting a malignant influence

midden – a mound or deposit containing shells, animal bones and other refuse that indicates the site of a human settlement

miz-maze – forms a pattern unlike conventional mazes as it has no junctions or crossings and the pattern is arranged like a very long rope neatly arranged to fit the area

motte and bailey – the predecessor of the castle, having a raised earth mound (motte) topped with a tower and a wooden ring fortification surrounding a courtyard (bailey)

oolite – a variety of limestone consisting of small round grains

Otherworld – the realm of the dead and of deities and spirits, a place where time does not exist. Some say it exists right alongside the world of the living but is invisible to most humans. In Ireland it is known, amongst other names, as Tir Na Og, the Land of the Young

outré – unconventional, eccentric or bizarre

Sabbath – a meeting of witches to practise witchcraft and sorcery

sarsen – a large sandstone boulder often found scattered over the English chalk downs. Such a stone used in a megalithic monument

'sensitives' – having the sense of feeling; possessing the capacity of receiving impressions from external objects and atmospheres

Sheela-na-Gig – a quasi-erotic stone carving of a female figure sometimes found on Norman or Romanesque churches

tor – a rocky peak or hill. A prominent rock or heap of rocks

'Traditionals' – witches who claim descent from early Pictish times and who have strong links with their local countryside

Tuatha de Danaan – the name means 'people of Danu'. Danu was an Irish goddess. They are a race of people found in Irish mythology, thought to derive from the pre-Christian deities of Ireland

tumulus – from the Latin 'mound or small hill'. Also known as *barrow*

votive – a ritual object given as an offering or used as a link to a spirit or deity

Wicca – derived from the Saxon *wicca* meaning sorcerer. Wicce is the female equivalent. Another word for witchcraft

wyrd wisdom – Anglo-Saxon spiritual teachings where all is seen as linked, as in a web. A wisdom connected to the landscape and life upon it. A way of knowledge practised by native shamans and used for healing, prophecy and protection for the tribe

Index

OTHER ROVING PRESS TITLES

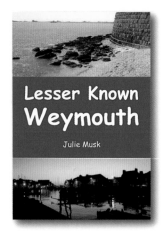

Lesser Known **Weymouth**

Julie Musk

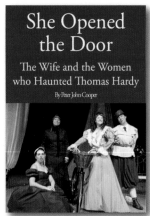

She Opened the Door

The Wife and the Women who Haunted Thomas Hardy

By Peter John Cooper

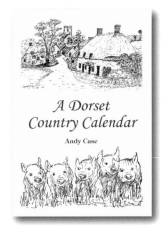

A Dorset Country Calendar

Andy Case

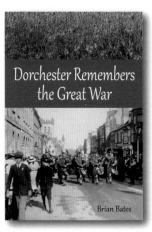

Dorchester Remembers the Great War

Brian Bates

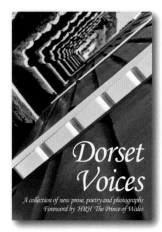

Dorset Voices

A collection of new prose, poetry and photographs
Foreword by HRH The Prince of Wales

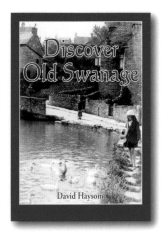

Discover Old Swanage

David Haysom

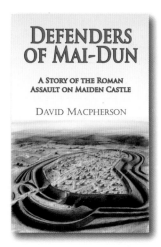

DEFENDERS OF MAI-DUN

A STORY OF THE ROMAN ASSAULT ON MAIDEN CASTLE

DAVID MACPHERSON

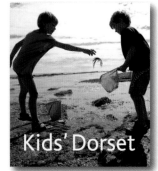

Kids' Dorset

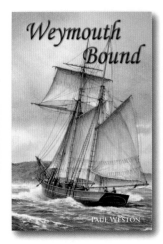

Weymouth Bound

PAUL WESTON

Roving Press

If you like exploring, you'll love our books